Collins
English for Exams

Cambridge English

First

Four Practice Tests

for Cambridge English: First (FCE)

Collins

HarperCollins Publishers
1 London Bridge Street
London SE1 9GF

First edition 2015

10 9 8 7 6 5 4 3 2 1

© HarperCollins Publishers 2015

ISBN 978-0-00-752954-4

Collins® is a registered trademark of HarperCollins Publishers Limited

www.collinselt.com

A catalogue record for this book is available from the British Library

Typeset in India by Aptara

Printed in China by South China Printing Co. Ltd

Author: Peter Travis

Illustrators: Aptara

Audio recordings by Dsound and SEA Studios

Photo credits

pii: **Peter Bernik**/Shutterstock; pii: **Darengphoto**/Shutterstock; piii: **Monkey Business Images**/Shutterstock; piii: **Dawn Shearer-Simonetti**/Shutterstock; pvi: **CREATISTA**/Shutterstock; pvi: **Zurijeta**/Shutterstock; pvii: **Pavel L Photo and Video**/Shutterstock; pvii: **l i g h t p o e t**/Shutterstock; px: **Pavel L Photo and Video**/Shutterstock; px: **Monkey Busienss Images**/Shutterstock; pgxi: **Goodluz**/Shutterstock; pxi: **wavebreakmedia**/Shutterstock; pxiv: **Photosky**/Shutterstock; pxiv: **Aleksandr Markin**/Shutterstock; pxv: **Beata Wawrzyniuk**/Shutterstock; pxv: **Pichugin Dmitry**/Shutterstock.

Contents

Introduction

About this book

Who is this book for?

This book will help you to prepare for the *Cambridge English: First* examination, also known as the *First Certificate in English* or *FCE*. This book will be useful if you are preparing for the exam for the first time or taking it again. The book and online training module have been designed so that you can use them to study on your own. However, you can also use the book if you are preparing for *Cambridge English: First* in a class.

Content

The book contains:

- **Tips for success** – essential advice for success in the exam
- **Guide to *Cambridge English: First*** – a guide to the exam
- **Quick guides** – easy-to-read guides with brief summaries of the different parts of each paper; these will help you to understand what you need to know in order to answer the questions correctly
- **Challenges and solutions** – advice to help you with common problems in each paper
- **Practice tests** – four complete practice tests with authentic test questions to help you to familiarise yourself with the exam
- **Mini-dictionary** – definitions of difficult words from the practice tests in this book (the definitions are from Collins COBUILD dictionaries)
- **Audio script** – the texts of what you hear in the Listening paper
- **Sample answer sheets** – make sure you know what the answer sheets for Papers 1, 2 and 3 look like
- **Answer key** – the answers for the Reading and Use of English papers and the Listening papers
- **Model answers** – examples of good answers for the Writing papers and the Speaking papers
- **CDs** – MP3 files with all the recordings for the Listening papers as well as model answers for the Speaking papers
- **Access code for online test and training module** – online practice tests with tips and advice to help you to improve your skills

Tips for success

Make a plan to succeed and start by following these tips.

- **Register for the exam early.** If you are studying on your own, use the Cambridge English website to find your local exam centre. Register as early as you can to give yourself plenty of time to prepare.

- **Start studying early.** The more you practise, the better your English will become. Give yourself at least one month to revise and complete all the practice tests in this book. Spend at least one hour a day studying.
- **Time yourself when you do the practice tests.** This will help you to feel more confident when you do the real exam.
- **Do every part in each practice test.** Do not be afraid to make notes on the book itself. For example, writing down the meaning of words you do not know on the book will help you to remember the words later on.
- For the Writing paper, **keep practising until you can write full answers** within the time limit.

Using the book for self-study

If you have not studied for *Cambridge English: First* before, it is recommended that you work through all the practice tests in this book in order. If you have a teacher or friend who can help you with speaking and writing, that would be very useful. It is also a good idea to study with other students who are preparing for the exam or who want to improve their English. Having a study partner will help you to keep motivated. You can also help each other with areas of English you might find difficult. However, even if you work alone, you can still learn a lot.

Begin preparing for *Cambridge English: First* by getting to know the different parts of each paper, what each part tests, and how many marks there are for each part. Use the information in this introduction as well as the *Quick guides* to find out all you can. You can also download the *Cambridge English: First Handbook* from the Cambridge English website for more details about the exam. There is a link to the website on page 7.

You need to know how to prepare for each of the papers in the best way possible. This is where the *Challenges and solutions* section of this book will be useful. Try to do the suggested activities as these will help you to develop the skills you need in order to do well in the exam.

When you are ready to try the practice tests, make sure you always attempt the tasks in the Writing papers and the Speaking papers. You can improve your writing and speaking skills only through regular and thorough practice. Practise writing to a time limit. If you find this difficult at first, start by writing a good answer of the correct length without worrying about time. Then start to reduce the time gradually until you can write an acceptable answer within the time limit. You should become familiar enough with your handwriting so that you can accurately estimate the number of words you have written without counting them. Study the model answers at the back of the book. They will give you a good idea of what your own answers should be like. Do not try to memorise answers to the questions in the Speaking papers. If you study hard and do all the practice tests in this book, you should learn the language you need to give good answers in the real exam.

Finally, read as much as possible in English as this is the best way to learn new vocabulary and improve your English.

Online test and training module

You can also prepare for the test online by working through the online test and training module. This contains two of the tests from the book. You can take one of the tests as practice for the computer-based version of the test. The other test forms part of the training module, which contains a test with added tips, advice and information to help you improve your skills. The training module also has additional practice material, so that you can work on areas that will help you get a better mark. The online test and training module will help you prepare for both the paper-based test and the computer-based test.

For information on how to access the training module, please turn to the back of the book.

About *Cambridge English: First*

In January 2015 an updated version of the exam will be introduced. The practice tests in this book follow the specifications of the new exam and will fully prepare you for taking the exam from January 2015. For more information, please go to www.cambridgeenglish.org.

Who is *Cambridge English: First* for?

Cambridge English: First is an upper-intermediate-level English exam run by Cambridge English, also known as Cambridge ESOL. It is for people who want to work in an English-speaking environment, to study at an upper-intermediate level such as on foundation or pathway courses, or to live independently in an English-speaking county. The exam can be taken on computer or as a paper-based exam.

The level of *Cambridge English: First*

Cambridge English: First is one of five Main Suite exams offered by Cambridge English.

- Cambridge English: Proficiency (CPE)
- Cambridge English: Advanced (CAE)
- **Cambridge English: First (FCE)**
- Cambridge English: Preliminary (PET)
- Cambridge English: Key (KET)

The table below shows how FCE fits into the Cambridge English Main Suite examinations. The level of FCE is described as being at B2 on the Common European Framework of Reference.

Proficient User	C2	CPE
	C1	CAE
Independent user	**B2**	**FCE**
	B1	PET
Basic User	A2	KET
	A1	

The papers of *Cambridge English: First*

There are four papers in the exam.

- Paper 1: Reading and Use of English (1 hour and 15 minutes)
- Paper 2: Writing (1 hour and 20 minutes)
- Paper 3: Listening (about 40 minutes, plus 5 minutes for transferring answers to the answer sheet)
- Paper 4: Speaking (14 minutes)

Timetabling

Papers 1, 2 and 3 are taken on the same day and in the order listed above. Paper 4: Speaking can be taken a few days before or after the other papers. If you are studying on your own, you should contact your exam centre for dates.

Marking

The Reading and Use of English paper is worth 40% of the total mark, and the Writing, Listening and Speaking papers are each worth 20% of the total mark.

Paper 1: Reading and Use of English has seven parts and a total of 52 questions.
Parts 1, 2 and 3 have eight questions each. There is one mark for each question.
Part 4 has six questions. There are up to two marks for each question.
Parts 5 and 6 have six questions each. There are two marks for each question.
Part 7 has ten questions. There is one mark for each question.

Paper 2: Writing has two parts.
Part 1 has one compulsory question.
In Part 2 you have to answer one question from a choice of three.
Each part has equal marks.

Part 3: Listening has four parts and a total of 30 questions.
Part 1 has eight questions.
Part 2 has ten questions.
Part 3 has five questions.
Part 4 has seven questions.
There is one mark for each question.

Part 4: Speaking has four parts. You will be assessed on your performance throughout.

You will receive a score on the Cambridge English Scale for each of the four skills and Use of English. You will also receive a score and a grade for your overall performance in the test:
Grade A: score 180–190
Grade B: score 170–180
Grade C: score 160–170

If you achieve a Grade A, you will receive a certificate stating that you have demonstrated ability at C1 level. If you achieve a Grade B or C, you will be awarded a *First Certificate in English* at B2 level. If your performance is below B2 level, but within B1, you will receive a certificate stating that you have demonstrated ability at B1 level.

For full details of how the exam is scored and marked, download the *Cambridge English: First Handbook* at: www.cambridgeenglish.org

READING AND USE OF ENGLISH

Quick guide

What is it?

The Reading section of the Reading and Use of English paper tests your ability to understand different types of texts on a variety of subjects. The Use of English section tests your ability to understand and use B2-level vocabulary and grammatical structures.

Skills needed

In order to do well in the Reading and Use of English paper, you must be able to:

- recognise and understand B2-level vocabulary including phrasal verbs, idioms, collocations and fixed phrases.
- understand and use a good range of B2-level grammatical structures.
- form words from other words using prefixes, suffixes, etc.
- read real-world texts such as extracts from fiction and non-fiction books, journals, articles and magazines, and understand main ideas, gist, details, opinions, attitudes, inferences, paraphrases, etc.
- understand how a text is organised.
- answer questions within the given time.

Paper 1: Reading and Use of English

The Reading and Use of English paper has seven parts.

Part 1 (multiple-choice cloze) has a short text with eight gaps. You have to complete the gaps by choosing the correct word from four options, A, B, C or D. This part focuses on vocabulary. (Total marks: 8)

Part 2 (open cloze) has a short text with eight gaps. You have to complete the gaps with one word in each space. This part focuses mainly on grammar but there is also some focus on vocabulary. (Total marks: 8)

Part 3 (word formation) has a short text with eight gaps. You have to complete each gap with a word formed from a word next to the line with the gap. This part focuses on vocabulary. (Total marks: 8)

Part 4 (key word transformation) has six questions. Each question has a pair of sentences. The second sentence in each pair has a gap and there is a given 'key' word. You have to complete the gap with two to five words including the 'key' word so that the sentence has the same meaning as the first sentence. This part focuses on grammar and vocabulary. (Total marks: 12)

Part 5 (multiple choice) has a text with six questions. You have to answer each question by choosing the correct answer from four options, A, B, C or D. This part focuses on understanding main idea, gist, detail, opinion, attitude, tone, purpose, meaning from context, implication and text organisation features. (Total marks: 12)

Part 6 (gapped text) has a text from which six sentences have been removed. The sentences appear in jumbled order at the end of the text. You have to complete the text by choosing the correct sentence for each gap. This part focuses on understanding cohesion, coherence and text structure. (Total marks: 12)

Part 7 (multiple matching) has one longer text or several shorter texts with ten questions or prompts. You have to match each question or prompt with one of the sections of the longer text or with one of the shorter texts, A, B, C or D. This part focuses on understanding detail, opinion, specific information and implication. (Total marks: 10)

Challenges and solutions

» **CHALLENGE 1: 'I don't know a lot of the words in the texts and questions.'**

SOLUTION: Use a learner's dictionary like the *Collins COBUILD Illustrated Intermediate Dictionary of English* when you study to help you to build your vocabulary. You should also use *Collins COBUILD Key Words for Cambridge English: First*. In this book there is a mini-dictionary with definitions of difficult words from the practice tests.

SOLUTION: Read English texts as often as possible. Read a range of text types including fiction and non-fiction books, newspapers, magazines and blogs. Do not worry about understanding every word but try to get a general understanding. If there are sections that cause difficulty, look up the meaning of any words that prevent understanding.

SOLUTION: Do not try to record all the new words or phrases you come across. Try to focus on high-frequency or common vocabulary.

SOLUTION: Use 'key' words and phrases that appear before and after unknown words to help you to guess their meaning. Read the sentence with the unknown word carefully. You may also need to read the whole paragraph in order to work out the meaning. In the table below there are some ideas for how key words and phrases might help you to understand a word. The unknown word is <u>underlined</u>.

Guessing the meaning of unknown words		
Ideas	**Key words and phrases**	**Examples**
Pay attention to examples near the unknown word. If you understand the examples, you can use them to guess the meaning of the unknown word.	*such as* *including* *this includes* *like* *for instance/example*	*The students had different <u>excuses</u> for not doing their homework, **such as** 'My dog ate it' or 'My mum washed it in the washing machine'.*

Guessing the meaning of unknown words		
Ideas	**Key words and phrases**	**Examples**
Look for key words that show the writer is contrasting two ideas. The unknown word might have the opposite meaning to the idea expressed in the sentence before or after it.	*but* *while* *Unlike X, . . .* *On the other hand, X . . .* *However, . . .*	*There is going to be a* <u>*heat wave*</u> *all this week.* ***However****, the weather will be much colder next week.*

SOLUTION: Prefixes and suffixes can help you to guess the meaning of unknown words. A prefix is one or more letters, e.g. *un-, dis-, pre-, co-, under-*, that go at the beginning of a word, e.g. <u>un</u>happy, <u>dis</u>organised. A suffix is one or more letters, e.g. *-ful, -less, -ation, -y, -ment, -hood*, that go at the end of a word, e.g. enjoy<u>ment</u>, neighbour<u>hood</u>. If you learn the meanings and uses of English prefixes and suffixes, you will be able to guess the meaning of many unknown words. For example, the prefixes *un-* and *dis-* give a word a negative meaning.

» **CHALLENGE 2: 'In Part 1 more than one choice seems correct to me.'**

SOLUTION: Part 1 tests your knowledge of vocabulary and in particular set expressions like phrasal verbs, idioms and collocations. Pay attention to the words before and after the gap because they may be part of a set expression. While you are studying for the exam, keep a record of vocabulary 'chunks' rather than just individual words and make a note of any interesting ones you come across in your reading.

SOLUTION: Skip the gaps you do not know and come back to them later. Cross out the answer options that you know are wrong so you have fewer options to choose from.

» **CHALLENGE 3: 'I can't decide what the missing words are in Part 2.'**

SOLUTION: Most gaps need a 'grammar' word. These are words such as determiners (e.g. *a, the, much, many*), prepositions (e.g. *on, at, in*) and conjunctions (e.g. *and, but, because*). Make a list of all the types of grammar words you find in practice tests and make sure you understand how they are used.

SOLUTION: Some gaps need words that are part of a set expression. For example, a text might have the expressions *at least* and *spend time*, and *at* and *spend* are in the gaps. Focus on the words around a gap and decide if the missing word is part of a set expression.

» **CHALLENGE 4: 'I always score badly in Part 3.'**

SOLUTION: Make a section in your vocabulary notebook for word forms and practise forming words from some of the words you find. For example:

Noun	Verb	Adjective	Adverb
belief believer	believe	(un)believable	(un)believably

SOLUTION: Read the text before completing any gaps. Identify what kind of word is missing: noun, verb, adjective or adverb. If it is a noun, should it be singular or plural? If it is a verb, what form of verb do you need? Does the word need to have a positive or negative meaning?

» **CHALLENGE 5: 'How can I learn all the different transformations for Part 4?'**

SOLUTION: Although it is impossible to predict which transformations will appear in the exam, there are some grammatical structures that are frequently tested. For example, you will often find a transformation from active to passive or from direct to indirect speech. As you do the practice tests in this book, pay attention to the types of grammar that are tested and revise any you find difficult.

» **CHALLENGE 6: 'I often don't have enough time to answer all the questions in Parts 5, 6 and 7.'**

SOLUTION: Read the text quickly using skimming and scanning skills to find the answers to questions. Skimming is when you read a text quickly, paying attention only to the most important ideas. In this way, you can often quickly find the important sections that many questions are based on. This will save you a lot of time. To be good at skimming, make sure you know where to find the most important ideas in a text. In the table below there is some information on where to find important ideas.

Part of the text	Skimming strategy
Titles/Headings	Read the title of a text; this sometimes gives you an idea of what the text is about. In the same way, paragraph headings may help you to find the topic of each paragraph.
Introduction	Read the last two or three sentences of the introductory paragraph. They often include the main idea of the text.
Main paragraphs	Read the first and last sentence of a paragraph. They usually include the main idea of the paragraph.
Conclusion	Read the first two or three sentences of the conclusion. They often say in a few words what the text was about.

Scanning is when you read a text quickly in order to find specific key words or ideas. After you have read a question and its answer options, you should make a note of any key words or ideas such as names or numbers. Then scan the text, looking specifically for those key words or ideas. The answers appear in the texts in the same order as the questions so if you have found the part of the text that answers a question, the part of the text that answers the next question must be below that part.

To practise skimming and scanning, find an article in a newspaper or magazine. First, skim the article and write down the most important ideas on a piece of paper. Then scan it for key words or ideas such as names or numbers. The more you practise skimming and scanning, the better you will become so try to practise every day.

SOLUTION: Time yourself when you do the practice tests and look at your watch occasionally. Do not spend too long on any one question; if you cannot answer it, carry on to the next question. This will help you not to get stuck on a question and waste your time.

» **CHALLENGE 7: 'The texts in Parts 5 and 6 are complicated and confusing. I get lost while I'm reading them.'**

SOLUTION: Look for 'signposts' as you read. These might be words that connect the ideas. For example, some words signal the introduction of a new topic (e.g. *Another example of X is* ...), while others signal a series of events (e.g. *First, ... Second, ... Finally, ...*). There are often 'signposts' at the beginning of a new paragraph although they can occur in the middle of a paragraph as well. If you understand how 'signposts' are used, you might be able to get a better idea of what the text is saying.

» **CHALLENGE 8: 'None of the answer options in Parts 5 and 7 "feel" right.'**

SOLUTION: Correct answer options express the key information in the text but usually use different words or 'paraphrase' to express it. Information can be paraphrased by using synonyms (words with a similar meaning) or a different grammatical structure (e.g. active to passive, or vice versa). Sometimes, the text gives details but the correct answer option expresses this key information in general terms. Be careful: the same words that appear in the text can also appear in an answer option. However, this does not mean that this option is correct. Such options often do not answer the question correctly.

SOLUTION: Cross out any answer options that are clearly incorrect. You are more likely to answer the question correctly if you have fewer options to choose from.

SOLUTION: Look for evidence of the answer in the text. For example, if you think an answer option is correct, find the part of the text where the answer appears, underline it and read it carefully. Make sure you are not just matching words in the answer option with words in the text, or that only part of the answer is correct. This is important in Part 7, where you have to match prompts with sections of a text: a text may have some of the necessary information but not all.

SOLUTION: The answers to the questions in Part 5 usually appear one after the other in the text. For example, you will find the answer to the second question after the answer to the first.

» **CHALLENGE 9: 'I find it difficult to identify the writer's opinion.'**

SOLUTION: Occasionally, a question might ask why the writer wrote the text or what the writer's opinion is on a subject. You could try answering such questions last, when you have a better understanding of the whole text.

SOLUTION: Read articles in magazines and newspapers. Do not worry about understanding every word; such articles will be at a fairly high level. Try to get a general idea of what the article is about and why the writer might have written it.

WRITING

Quick guide

What is it?

The Writing paper tests your ability to write an appropriate, well-organised response to a question using the correct register and format, and a good range of B2-level vocabulary and grammatical structures.

Skills needed

In order to do well in the Writing paper, you must be able to:

- understand the instructions and include all the key points in your answer.
- write a range of formal and informal texts such as essays, articles, letters, emails, reports and reviews.
- use an appropriate register and format.
- write a well-organised text that is easy for the reader to follow.
- use a good range of B2-level vocabulary and grammatical structures.
- write your answers within the word limits given in the instructions.
- write your answers within the given time.

Paper 2: Writing

The Writing paper has two parts.

Part 1 is compulsory. You have to write an essay in 140–190 words, expressing your opinion on a given essay title. You are given some ideas which you have to include in your answer, and you must also include an idea of your own.

In **Part 2** you have to answer one question in 140–190 words from a choice of three. The possible text types are an article, an email, a letter, a report or a review.

Challenges and solutions

CHALLENGE 1: 'I'm not sure how much time to spend on each question.'

SOLUTION: Know how much time you have. On the day of the exam, wear a watch. While you work, keep an eye on the time. You can use this guide while you write.

Part 1: Total time: 40 minutes	
Time	What you should do
about 8 minutes	Read the instructions carefully and plan your essay.
about 25 minutes	Write your essay. Make sure you include the ideas you are given as well as your own idea.
about 7 minutes	Check your essay carefully for mistakes (e.g. grammar, spelling, punctuation, word order).

Part 2: Total time: 40 minutes	
about 3 minutes	Read all three questions carefully and decide which question you can answer best.
about 5 minutes	Read the instructions of the question you are going to answer again. Underline the key words and think carefully about the register and format you need to use. Then plan your writing.
about 25 minutes	Write your answer.
about 7 minutes	Check your writing carefully for mistakes (e.g. grammar, spelling, punctuation, word order).

» **CHALLENGE 2: 'I'm afraid the examiner will not understand my ideas.'**

SOLUTION: Use 'transition' words that connect the ideas in two sentences. They make your writing easier to understand. In the table below there are some examples.

Function	Transition words
To contrast or change focus	*but Conversely, … despite/in spite of However, …* *In contrast, … Nevertheless, … Nonetheless, …* *On the contrary, … On the other hand, … though yet*
To add	*Additionally, … also and Besides that, …* *Furthermore, … In addition, … Moreover, …*
To come to a conclusion	*As a result, … Consequently, … For that reason, …* *Therefore, …*
To clarify	*in other words namely that is to say*
To show sequence	*after as soon as before Finally, … First/Second/Third,* *… later meanwhile next soon then*

SOLUTION: Practise your spelling. While a few misspelled words will not affect your score, a lot of spelling mistakes may prevent the examiner from understanding your writing easily. One way to improve your spelling is to read a lot: the more often you see words in English, the more easily you will remember how they are spelled.

» **CHALLENGE 3: 'I'm not sure how the different text types are organised.'**

SOLUTION: It is important to be familiar with each of the text types you need to be able to write. Download the *Cambridge English: First Handbook* from the Cambridge English website. The Writing section has several sample answers with comments by an examiner. These will give you an idea of what each text type looks like and how it should be organised.

SOLUTION: Whichever text type you are writing, organise it clearly using paragraphs. If you find it difficult to use paragraphs, pay attention to the paragraphs in the texts you read. See if you can identify the topic of each paragraph. Can you find the topic sentence? How is the paragraph organised? How do the rest of the sentences relate to the topic sentence?

» **CHALLENGE 4: 'I don't know what to write about in Part 1.'**

SOLUTION: The essay question in Part 1 will give you two ideas to use in your answer. In order to come up with more ideas, brainstorm the topic: think about the topic and spend a minute or two writing down all the points you can think of for different sides of the argument. When you have finished brainstorming, you can look at the notes you have made and choose the best points.

SOLUTION: In Part 1 there are no right or wrong opinions. In other words, you are not being tested on your opinions. The important thing is how well you express yourself and support your opinion.

SOLUTION: Make a list of the essay topics in this book and any other practice tests you come across. Try coming up with ideas for each topic and give yourself about two to three minutes to do so. In this way, you will get used to thinking of ideas in a limited time.

» **CHALLENGE 5: 'I don't know if I can express an opinion in Part 2.'**

SOLUTION: You need to express agreement or disagreement in Part 1 and also give reasons for your opinion. But you might also need to express your opinion in a letter or email, a report or a review in Part 2. Here are examples of expressions you can use.

- *It seems to me that ...*
- *As far as I am concerned, ...*
- *In my opinion, ...*
- *My view is that ...*
- *I agree/disagree with the idea that ...*
- *I agree/disagree with X to some extent.*
- *While some people think that ..., I believe that ...*
- *Other people might disagree, but my view is that ...*
- *I know that some people feel differently, but it is my opinion that ...*

» **CHALLENGE 6: 'I have difficulty writing formal letters.'**

SOLUTION: Keep a record of set expressions often found in formal letters such as letters of complaint, letters requesting information or letters of application. In the table below there are some examples of such expressions. Add more as you come across them.

Part of letter	Set expressions
Beginning	*I am writing with reference/regards to ...* *With reference to (your letter/advertisement), ...*
Main body	*Please find enclosed ...* *I would be grateful if you could ...*
End	*I look forward to hearing from you soon.* *I hope this information is useful.* *Do not hesitate to contact me should you require any further information.*

» CHALLENGE 7: 'I have difficulty writing informal letters or emails.'

SOLUTION: There are many set expressions that native speakers use to begin and end informal letters or emails or to comment on something. Learn as many of these expressions as you can. In the table below there are some examples of such expressions. Add more as you come across them.

Part of letter	Set expressions
Beginning	*How are you? I hope you're well.* *Thanks for your letter. It was great to hear from you.*
Commenting on information	*I'm sorry to hear … I'm so pleased to hear …* *It's great to hear …*
Ending	*Write back soon. Best wishes,* *See you soon. Take care.*

SOLUTION: Keep a record of examples of informal and formal language that you could use in your writing. In the table below there are some examples of such language. Add more as you come across them.

	Informal	Formal
Contractions	*I'm / You're / It's*	*I am / You are / It is*
Vocabulary	*I'm up to my ears in work.* *put up with*	*I am very busy.* *tolerate*
Tone	*I was really angry when I discovered …*	*I was rather disappointed to discover …*
Grammar	Active	Passive Inversion (e.g. *Should you … Had I …*)

» CHALLENGE 8: 'I'm not sure how to improve my vocabulary for the exam.'

SOLUTION: Practise paraphrasing (saying the same things using different words). Choose a text from a Reading and Use of English paper in this book. Then choose a paragraph and read it carefully. Close the book and try to paraphrase what you have read. When you have finished, compare your paragraph with the one in the book. Did you change key words by using synonyms (words with the same meaning)? Did you change structures (e.g. active to passive)? Practising paraphrasing is a good way to improve your vocabulary.

LISTENING

Quick guide

What is it?

The Listening paper tests your comprehension of conversations, talks, recorded messages and broadcasts.

Skills needed

In order to do well in the Listening paper, you must be able to:
- understand main ideas, details and specific information.
- identify feeling, attitude, opinion, purpose and agreement between speakers.
- answer questions within the given time.

Paper 3: Listening

The Listening paper has four parts.

Part 1 (multiple choice) has eight short extracts (about 30 seconds) from conversations, recorded messages or radio broadcasts, and eight questions. For each question, you have to listen and choose the correct answer from three options, A, B or C. This part focuses on gist, detail, specific information, feeling, attitude, opinion, purpose and agreement between speakers. (Total marks: 8)

Part 2 (sentence completion) has a longer monologue (3–4 minutes) and ten questions. You have to listen and complete ten sentences with information from the recording. This part focuses on gist, detail, specific information and stated opinion. (Total marks: 10)

Part 3 (multiple matching) has five short unrelated monologues (about 30 seconds) and five questions. You have to listen and choose the correct option from a list of eight. This part focuses on main points, gist, detail, feeling, attitude, opinion and purpose. (Total marks: 5)

Part 4 (multiple choice) has an interview or an exchange between two speakers (3–4 minutes) and seven questions. You have to listen and choose the correct answer from three options, A, B or C. This part focuses on main idea, gist, detail, specific information, attitude and opinion. (Total marks: 7)

Challenges and solutions

» **CHALLENGE 1: 'I don't understand a lot of the words in the recordings and the questions.'**

SOLUTION: The basic instructions for the parts of the Listening paper are always the same so by listening to the recordings in this book, you will know exactly what you have to do in the real exam. The instructions are also written on the exam paper so you can follow what is said. You will hear the recording for each part twice so if you do not understand something the first time, listen for it again the second time.

SOLUTION: After the instructions for Parts 2, 3 and 4 there will be a pause to give you the chance to read the questions. This is very useful. By reading the questions first, you will get an idea of what the recording will be about and you can guess what the answers might be. You will also have time to find the key words so that you can listen for the right answers.

SOLUTION: The recordings often provide a clue to the meaning of key words. In the table below there are some examples.

Guessing the meaning of unknown words	
Clues	**Example**
Repetition: The speaker repeats a key word in different sentences.	*Many animals use* **camouflage** *to protect themselves from predators. There are good examples of such* **camouflage** *amongst the insects. The* **camouflage** *used by stick insects, for example, ...*
Re-wording: The speaker rewords a phrase so that the meaning is clearer. He/She might use an expression like the following: *By that, I mean ...; What I'm talking about here is ...; In other words, ...*	*Why do companies vet new hires?* **By that, I mean** *why do they perform background checks and check out the potential employee's history?*
Definitions: The speaker might use an expression like the following to introduce a definition: *This refers to ...; This means ...; That's a ...; I think a definition is in order here.*	*It's a matter of agency.* **I think a definition is in order here**. *Agency is people's ability to make choices that will influence their futures.*
Giving examples: The speaker might clarify a word by giving examples which he/she might introduce by using an expression like the following: *like; such as; for instance/example.*	*Engaging in recreational activities* **such as** *jogging or playing an instrument has been shown to reduce stress levels.*

» **CHALLENGE 2: 'I get lost when I listen to the monologue in Part 2.'**

SOLUTION: The questions follow the order of the information in the recording. Use the pause before the first listening to read all the questions. Underline key words and listen for them when the recording starts. Using the questions as a guide in this way will help you not to get lost when you listen.

SOLUTION: Listen for 'signposts' (words or phrases that signal that the speaker is going give a particular type of information). Some 'signposts' signal the introduction of a new topic (e.g. *Next, ...; Turning now to ...*). Others signal the definition of a word (e.g. *By that, I mean ...*). If you listen for 'signposts', you can get a better idea of what the speaker is saying, which will help you to stay focused. To practise, listen to the recordings in this book and write down all the 'signpost' words you hear. Then check your notes against the audio script. How many did you notice?

» **CHALLENGE 3: 'I often write too many words when I complete the sentences in Part 2.'**

SOLUTION: You should try to complete each sentence with a single word, a short phrase or a number. Do not write more than this. The missing words are the same as ones you will hear in the recording; you do not have to write a different word or number. However, the words you read around the gap may not be in the same order or even the same words you hear in the recording. Therefore, it is important to listen for meaning and not just for the missing words.

» **CHALLENGE 4: 'In Parts 3 and 4, none of the options "feel" right, or more than one option seems to be correct.'**

SOLUTION: Correct answer options express the key information in the recording but usually paraphrase it by using synonyms (words with a similar meaning) or a different grammatical structure (e.g. active to passive). Sometimes, the recording gives details but the correct answer option expresses this information in general terms ('specific to general'). Here are some examples:

- **Synonyms**

You hear this:	*Could you give me a hand with my suitcase? It's a bit heavy.*
Question:	*You hear a conversation between a man and a woman. What does the woman want the man to do?*
Answer options:	*A help her with her luggage* ✓
	B hand her the suitcase
	C weigh her bag

- **'Specific to general'**

You hear this:	*The police officer asked me for my vehicle registration and driving licence.*
Question:	*What did the police officer want?*
Answer options:	*A to check the car*
	B to ask the man some questions
	C to see documentation ✓

But be careful: words that you hear in the recording can also appear in the answer options. However, this does not mean that the option is correct; such options often do not answer the question correctly. When you do the practice tests in this book, try to identify the paraphrase types in some of the answer options. This will help you to learn to recognise correct and incorrect answers.

SOLUTION: Read the answer options carefully and cross out the ones that are clearly incorrect or that do not answer the question. You are more likely to answer the question correctly if you have fewer options to choose from.

SOLUTION: Some questions ask you to identify a speaker's opinion or attitude. Learn the different expressions that speakers use when they give an opinion, e.g. *I think …; In my opinion, …; I feel … .*

SOLUTION: Do not spend too much time answering any one question. If you are not certain of an answer, choose the answer option that is the most appealing and move on to the next question. If you spend too long worrying about the correct answer, you might not hear the answer to the next question.

» **CHALLENGE 5: 'I don't always understand the speakers. Sometimes they talk too fast.'**

SOLUTION: Listen as much as possible to natural English. The more you listen to native English speech, the better you will understand the English used in the exam. Try the following:

- Watch TV programmes or films. The programmes do not have to be educational – comedies and dramas have good examples of natural English. If you find this difficult, watch English-language films with subtitles. Listening can be easier when you can read to check understanding.
- Join an English-language club. Your university, local library or community centre might have one. By joining, you will be able to practise speaking English and have the chance to hear native speakers.
- Join an online language community. There may be native speakers of English who want to learn your language and will be happy to practise talking to you using online tools like Skype.

SOLUTION: Download English-language podcasts or radio programmes that you can store on your computer. At first, practise listening for only a minute or two at a time. As your comprehension gets better, listen for a longer time. Listen as many times as you need to until you understand the main ideas.

SPEAKING

Quick guide

What is it?

The Speaking paper tests your ability to understand and use spoken English. You will take the Speaking paper with another candidate, although there is a small chance that you will take it with two other candidates.

Skills needed

In order to do well in the Speaking paper, you must be able to:

- understand and use the language of social interactions.
- describe and compare.
- express your opinion.
- discuss a subject and come to a decision.
- speak using a good range of B2-level vocabulary and grammatical structures.
- organise your thoughts and express them clearly.

Paper 4: Speaking

The Speaking paper has four parts.

In **Part 1** the examiner asks you some simple questions about your personal details, daily routine, past experiences, future plans, etc. This part focuses on general interaction and social language. (Time: 2–3 minutes)

In **Part 2** the examiner gives you two colour photographs and asks you to describe and compare what you can see. You have to speak for one minute. When you have finished, the examiner asks the other candidate to comment on your photographs. He/She has to speak for 30 seconds. Then the examiner gives the other candidate two different photographs on the same theme. When the other candidate has finished speaking, the examiner asks you to comment on the photographs. You have to speak for 30 seconds. This part focuses on describing, comparing, expressing opinions and organising speech. (Time: 4 minutes)

In **Part 3** the examiner gives you instructions and some written prompts and asks you and the other candidate to discuss a topic (two minutes) and then come to a decision about it (one minute). This part focuses on exchanging ideas, expressing and justifying opinions, agreeing and/or disagreeing, suggesting, speculating, evaluating, negotiating to reach a decision, etc. (Time: 4 minutes)

In **Part 4** the examiner asks you and the other candidate questions related to the topic of Part 3. This part focuses on expressing and justifying opinions, agreeing and/or disagreeing and speculating. (Time: 4 minutes)

Challenges and solutions

» **CHALLENGE 1: 'I'm not sure how much to say when I answer the examiner's questions in Part 1.'**

SOLUTION: This part is just a simple conversation between you and the examiner. It is a chance for him/her to get to know more about you. You do not have to give long answers but you should say more than 'Yes' or 'No'. When you answer Part 1 questions, give a reason for your answer or an example. For example:

Examiner: *What kind of food do you like to eat?*

Candidate: *I enjoy Indian food. There's a really nice restaurant near my house and I always order something spicy to eat when we go there.*

» **CHALLENGE 2: 'I'm not sure I'll have enough to say in Parts 1 and 4.'**

SOLUTION: The questions in Part 1 are about you and your experiences. The examiner might ask you to talk about your hobbies and interests, where you live, your family, your studies, etc. and you already know a lot about these subjects! Look at the table below. Think about the kind of questions the examiner might ask you about the subjects and how you would answer them.

Subjects	Possible questions
Where you live	*Do many tourists visit your town?*
Your hobbies or interests	*Have you always had the same hobbies and interests?*
Your friends and family	*Who do you look like in your family?*
Your daily routine	*What time do you like getting up?*
Your studies	*What was/is your favourite subject at school?*
Your favourite TV programmes/films/books/music	*Have you read a book lately that you really enjoyed?*
The food you like/do not like	*What kind of food do people in your country like to eat?*

SOLUTION: Try not to use the same words and phrases all the time. For example, the following expressions all mean *I like* or *I don't like*:

- *I quite fancy ...*
- *I'm quite fond of ...*
- *I've always been keen on ...*
- *I've got a soft spot for ...*
- *I'm (not) fond of ...*
- *I'm (not) keen on ...*
- *I (don't) enjoy ...*

- *I can't stand ...*
- *I'm (not) a big fan of ...*
- *I'm not that bothered about ...*
- *I can't bear ...*
- *X doesn't really appeal to me.*
- *I've never really fancied ...*

In the same way, do not keep using *I think*. Instead, try using a variety of expressions. Here are some examples:

- *As far as I'm concerned, ...*
- *As I see it, ...*
- *For my part, ...*
- *I don't really have an opinion one way or the other. I suppose ...*
- *I've always been of the opinion that ...*
- *If you ask me, ...*
- *In my view, ...*
- *It seems to me that ...*
- *It's not something I've given much thought to. Perhaps ...*
- *Speaking for myself, ...*
- *To my mind, ...*

SOLUTION: In Part 4 it is important to interact with the examiner and the other candidate naturally. You will gain marks if you ask the other candidate questions and respond to what he/she says. This means you must listen carefully to what he/she says.

SOLUTION: Practise using 'reply questions' appropriately. These are useful in Part 3 and Part 4 and you will gain marks for interacting naturally. Here are some examples:

A: *I used to play football for my school.*

B: **Did you?** *Were you good?*

A: *I've never eaten Spanish food.*

B: **Haven't you?** *It's really nice.*

> » **CHALLENGE 3: 'Sometimes I worry that I won't have enough time to finish talking in Part 2 and other times I worry that I won't have enough to say!'**

SOLUTION: Time yourself when you practise for Part 2 so that you get a good idea what it feels like to talk for one minute. Do the speaking tasks in this book and find more on the Internet. By timing yourself while you practise, you will learn not to speak too fast or too slowly and you will be able to give a complete answer within the time allowed.

> » **CHALLENGE 4: 'In Part 2 I'm worried that my description will be disorganised and I'll get into a mess.'**

SOLUTION: Practise using a structure for your description. Here is a suggestion:

- Begin by saying what the photograph is about. For example: *These photographs show people celebrating. The first one looks like a children's birthday party ...*
- Talk about any people in the photograph and what they are doing. For example: *There are lots of children and two adults. Some are sitting at a table and the adults are serving them food.* You could continue by describing what some of them are wearing or what they seem to be eating or doing.

- Do the same for the second photograph but remember to compare and contrast the two scenes. For example: *The second photo also shows people celebrating but this looks like a work-related occasion. In contrast with the first photograph, all the people are seated and ...*
- If you have time, finish by commenting on the scene. For example: *The first photograph reminds me of the birthday parties I had as a child.*

SOLUTION: There are many words and expressions that you can use to help you to organise your thoughts. In the table below there are some common examples. Add new words and expressions as you learn them.

Use	Words and expressions	
Comparing	*although* *but* *compared to*	*However, ...* *On the one hand, ...* *On the other hand, ...*
Giving reasons	*because* *because of*	*so* *in order to*
Giving examples	*for example* *for instance*	*To give you an example, ...*
Adding	*The first reason is ...* *The second reason is ...* *Also, ...*	*What's more, ...* *Finally, ...*
Concluding	*So all in all, ...* *To sum up, ...*	*In general, ...*

» **CHALLENGE 5: 'I'm worried that the examiners won't understand me. My pronunciation is bad.'**

SOLUTION: The examiner does not expect you to speak with a native speaker accent. In fact, having an accent is not regarded as a problem, even at a higher level. The important thing is to speak clearly so that people can understand you easily. Ask your friends to listen to a recording of you speaking English. They might be able to tell you about pronunciation problems you have. In particular, ask them if it is easy to understand what you are saying. What words do they have difficulty understanding? Practise saying the words you have the most trouble with.

SOLUTION: Record yourself speaking English. Download an English-language news programme or podcast. Listen to it and write out a few paragraphs. Then record yourself reading this transcription. Compare the recording of your voice with that of the native speaker. Can you imitate the pronunciation and intonation of the native speaker? Keep practising until you can.

SOLUTION: Practise speaking English with native English speakers. To find native English speakers in your area, try going to tourist attractions in your city. You could also join an English language club at your school. If your school does not have one, check at your local library or start one yourself!

SOLUTION: Some speakers have trouble with certain sounds. For example, Spanish speakers sometimes add *e* to English words beginning with *s*, e.g. 'eschool'. Other speakers pronounce the letter *w* as a *v*. Find out if speakers from your country have a particular problem with English pronunciation and practise that area.

SOLUTION: If you want people to understand you when you speak, you have to stress words correctly. If you stress the wrong syllable, people might not understand you. For example, in the following nouns, the underlined syllable is stressed:

- *cele<u>bra</u>tion*
- *ad<u>ver</u>tisement*
- *phot<u>og</u>raphy*

However, in the verb form, a different syllable is stressed:
- *<u>cel</u>ebrate*
- *<u>ad</u>vertise*
- *<u>phot</u>ograph*

Knowing how to pronounce words with more than one syllable is important and you should use a good dictionary to check the stress of any new words.

» **CHALLENGE 6: 'I don't know what to do if I realise I've made a mistake when I'm speaking.'**

SOLUTION: Correcting yourself when you make a mistake is a good way of showing the examiner that you do know the correct word or item of grammar. But you must also show that you can speak for quite a long time and this will be difficult if you correct yourself all the time. It is best to correct some mistakes but try to relax and speak as fluently as possible.

SOLUTION: Practise speaking English as much as you can before the exam. One way to do this is to speak to yourself when you are alone. The advantage of being alone is that you will be relaxed and less worried about making mistakes. Talk about what has happened during the day, what your plans are for the rest of the week or your opinion of anything that is in the news.

Test 1

PAPER 1 READING AND USE OF ENGLISH (1 hour 15 minutes)

Part 1

For questions **1–8**, read the text below and choose which answer (**A**, **B**, **C** or **D**) best completes each gap. Here is an example (**0**).

Example:

0	**A** mention	**B** refer	**C** talk	**D** specify

Answer:

0	A	B	C	D
	☐	■	☐	☐

The Hackney Cab

The words commonly used by Londoners to (**0**) .... to the black London taxi, their most famous (**1**) .... of transport, does, in fact, have international origins. The official name for the London taxi is 'hackney carriage', a term which comes from the French word 'hacquenée', meaning a general-purpose carriage that could be hired. The first hackney carriages (**2**) .... during the (**3**) .... of Queen Elizabeth I. These horse-drawn carriages belonged to wealthy aristocrats, who hired them out to less well-off (**4**) .... of the gentry. 'Cab', a shortened form of another French word, 'cabriolet', was the name given to the faster, two-wheeled carriages that were introduced from France during the nineteenth century. (**5**) .... the word 'taxi' has a European dimension. The 'taximeter' was an instrument invented by a German, Wilhelm Bruhn, in 1891. This machine (**6**) .... an end to debates about the cost of a cab ride as it measured the distance travelled and time taken of all (**7**) ...., allowing the driver to (**8**) .... the customer an accurate fare.

1   **A** system   **B** style   **C** mode   **D** manner

2   **A** appeared   **B** showed   **C** arose   **D** surfaced

3   **A** command   **B** control   **C** regime   **D** reign

4   **A** parts   **B** agents   **C** members   **D** individuals

5   **A** Even   **B** Still   **C** Like   **D** Since

6   **A** put   **B** made   **C** set   **D** left

7   **A** tours   **B** voyages   **C** travels   **D** journeys

8   **A** earn   **B** charge   **C** cost   **D** credit

Part 2

For questions **9–16**, read the text below and think of the word which best completes each gap. Use **one** word only in each gap. Here is an example (**0**).

Example: | 0 | H | O | W | | | | | | | | | | | | | | | | | |

Pokhora

It is difficult to describe just (**0**) .... beautiful the Himalayan city of Pokhora really is. Snowy mountain peaks serve as a backdrop to crystal-clear lakes surrounded by green forests.

Once a major trade route (**9**) .... India and Tibet, Pokhora is Nepal's second largest city. There are three main lakes in the area, (**10**) .... most popular of (**11**) .... is Phewa Lake. Tourists come here (**12**) .... their thousands to admire the mirror-like waters and relax amongst some truly spectacular scenery. Lakeside, a thriving resort town, (**13**) .... emerged along the eastern shore of the lake and offers visitors (**14**) .... wealth of hotels, restaurants and souvenir shops.

For those (**15**) .... want to get out and explore the countryside, bikes can (**16**) .... hired to explore the lush green fields and the gorgeous little villages or to cycle along river banks. Visitors can also take a boat to visit the island temple of Barahi, situated in the middle of Phewa Lake.

Part 3

For questions **17–24**, read the text below. Then use the word in capitals at the end of some of the lines to form a word that completes the gap in the same line. Here is an example (**0**).

Example:

0	F	A	S	H	I	O	N	A	B	L	E								

How Healthy Are Fish Pedicures?

In the past few years, fish pedicures have become very (**0**) .... These   **FASHION**

(**17**) .... involve a person placing their feet in a tank of water full of tiny   **TREAT**

Garra rufa fish. The fish nibble the person's feet, eating and removing the

dead skin. The benefits are said to be (**18**) ....: the pedicures seem   **NUMBER**

to stimulate blood flow and improve (**19**) ...., they make the skin   **CIRCULATE**

feel soft and clean, and they can help eliminate foot odour. Indeed, the

(**20**) .... of fish pedicures has exploded in the past few years and   **POPULAR**

dozens of centres have opened nationwide.

However, there have been reports claiming that there is a risk associated

with fish pedicures. Some health experts warn that there is a (**21**) ....   **POSSIBLE**

that people could pick up an (**22**) .... from the water, the fish or other   **INFECT**

patients' feet. Other experts claim the risk is small and that reports like

these (**23**) .... the problem. However, they do recommend that centres   **ESTIMATE**

undergo regular inspections to make sure the pedicures are not being

carried out in (**24**) .... conditions.   **HYGIENE**

Part 4

For questions **25–30**, complete the second sentence in each pair so that it has a similar meaning to the first sentence. Use the word in capitals. **Do not change the word in capitals.** You have to use between **two** and **five** words, including the word in capitals. Here is an example (**0**).

Example:

0   They would be happier leaving the party early.

PREFER

They .... the party early.

The gap can be completed by 'would prefer to leave' so write:

Answer: | **0** | | *WOULD PREFER TO LEAVE* |

Write **only** the missing words **IN CAPITAL LETTERS on your answer sheet**.

---

25   If you ask me, they should do something to lower the price of petrol.

CONCERNED

As .... , they should do something to lower the price of petrol.

26   I must say that I have never found football interesting.

INTEREST

I must say that I have never had .... football.

27   I only did the teaching course because I wanted to teach abroad.

ORDER

I only did the teaching course .... abroad.

28   My teacher recommended that I should buy an advanced dictionary.

IDEA

My teacher said that it would be .... an advanced dictionary.

29   I had a terrible headache and found it difficult to continue with my work.

GET

I found it difficult to .... my work as I had a terrible headache.

30   Provided you pay me back before the weekend, I'll lend you the money.

YOU

As .... me back before the weekend, I'll lend you the money.

Part 5

You are going to read an extract from a short story about a woman called Ma Parker. For questions **31–36**, choose the best answer (**A**, **B**, **C** or **D**) according to the text.

The Life of Ma Parker

When the literary gentleman, whose flat old Ma Parker cleaned every Tuesday, opened the door to her that morning, he asked after her grandson. Ma Parker stood on the doormat inside the dark little hall, and she stretched out her hand to help her gentleman shut the door before she replied. 'We buried him yesterday, sir.' Poor old bird. She did look heartbroken. 'I hope the funeral was a – a – success,' he said. Ma Parker gave no answer. She bent her head and hobbled off to the kitchen.

It would take a whole book to describe the state of that kitchen. During the week the literary gentleman 'did' for himself. That is to say, he emptied the tea leaves now and again into a jam jar set aside for that purpose, and if he ran out of clean forks, he wiped over one or two on the towel. Otherwise, as he explained to his friends, his 'system' was quite simple, and he couldn't understand why people made all this fuss about housekeeping.

'You simply dirty everything you've got, get someone in once a week to clean up, and the thing's done.'

The result looked like a gigantic dustbin. Even the floor was littered with toast crusts, envelopes, cigarette ends. But Ma Parker bore him no grudge. She pitied the poor gentleman for having no one to look after him. Out of the smudgy little window you could see an immense expanse of sad-looking sky, and whenever there were clouds, they looked very worn, old clouds, frayed at the edges, with holes in them or dark stains like tea.

While the water was heating, Ma Parker began sweeping the floor. 'Yes,' she thought, as the broom knocked, 'what with one thing and another I've had my share of misfortune. I've had a hard life.'

Even the neighbours said that of her. Many a time hobbling home, she heard them, waiting at the corner, or leaning over their fences, say among themselves, 'She's had a hard life, has Ma Parker.' It was true and she wasn't in the least proud of it. A hard life!

At sixteen she'd left Stratford and come up to London as a kitchen maid. Yes, she was born in Stratford-on-Avon. Shakespeare? People were always asking her about him. But she'd never heard his name until she saw it at the theatre.

Nothing remained in her memory of Stratford except 'sitting in the fireplace to see the stars through the chimney' and 'Mother always had her joint of meat hanging from the ceiling'. And there was something – a bush at the front door – that smelt ever so nice. But the bush was very vague. She'd only remembered it once or twice in the hospital, when she'd been taken bad.

And that was an awful place – her first place of work in London. She was never allowed out. She never went upstairs except for prayers morning and evening. And the cook was a cruel woman. She used to snatch away her letters from home before she'd read them and throw them in the fire because they made her dreamy. And the beetles! Would you believe it? Until she came to London, she'd never seen a black beetle. Here Ma always gave a little laugh. Not to have seen a black beetle! Well! It was as if you said you'd never seen your own feet.

When that family sold up, she worked as 'help' at a doctor's house, and after two years there, running around from morning till night, she'd married her husband.

31 What do we learn about Ma Parker in the first paragraph?

    A She doesn't like cleaning the man's house.

    B She is about to go to a funeral.

    C There has been a death in her family.

    D She works for a man who is ill.

32 What does the author suggest about the literary gentleman?

    A He never did anything for himself.

    B He didn't think housework was a problem.

    C He thought he was too important to do housework.

    D He always had enough clean forks.

33 Ma Parker

    A felt sorry for the man.

    B was shocked at how untidy the kitchen was.

    C was sad whenever she entered the kitchen.

    D wished the man had a wife.

34 Ma Parker's neighbours

    A annoyed her.

    B were worried about her.

    C understood what her life was like.

    D were proud of her.

35 The author mentions Stratford-on-Avon to show that

    A Ma Parker came from a theatrical background.

    B life there was completely different to life in London.

    C Ma Parker didn't have pleasant memories of living there.

    D Ma Parker's memories of the place were fading.

36 When Ma Parker thinks 'It was as if you said you'd never seen your own feet', she means

    A she thought the beetles were funny.

    B the beetles made cleaning the house unpleasant.

    C it was common to see beetles in London.

    D beetles were always getting under her feet.

Part 6

You are going to read an article about a man who is an expert at using a yo-yo. Six sentences have been removed from the article. Complete the gaps (**37–42**) in the article with the sentences **A–G**. There is one extra sentence that you do not need to use.

SPIN DOCTOR

In his youth, Lawrence Sayegh dreamt of performing in vaudeville, but his career took a different spin. He became nine-time world champion and international master trickster of … the yo-yo. He has wowed audiences in 26 countries, most states of the US, and on countless film and television screens. Today, at 64, he is still spinning, much to everyone's delight.

Sayegh says he was searching for a sport when he found the yo-yo. 'I was too short for basketball, too light for football, too nervous for baseball,' he says. **37** [ ] When the Duncan Yo-Yo Company began holding neighbourhood competitions in the 1940s, he won every contest within biking distance of his home. He became so good that Duncan eventually barred him from the contests.

His parents, however, were sceptical of their son's talent. 'They were both born in Damascus. They had a mom-and-pop grocery store and were very much of the old school: work, work, work; make something of yourself,' he says. The yo-yo didn't seem to offer a career path for Larry. But after he graduated from high school, the president of Duncan Yo-Yo contacted Sayegh and offered him a job. **38** [ ]

Duncan sent its new recruit off to demonstrate the company's product in the South and Southwest of the United States, and in Europe. In 1952, the company showed Sayegh off at a press conference in Paris. At the time, Sayegh says, the yo-yo was even more popular in Europe than in the US. **39** [ ] He was a huge hit. *Actualités*, the French newsreel played in movie houses before the feature, filmed Sayegh and his yo-yo tricks in settings all around Paris and put him onscreen all over the country.

Two years later, Sayegh won his first world championship in another competition sponsored by Duncan. Over the next eight years, until Duncan went out of business and the contest folded with the company, he won every year. In 1958, Ford Motor Company demonstrated its product's unbeatably smooth ride to prospective buyers in Australia by filming Sayegh, yo-yos spinning, atop the roof of a moving car in Tasmania. Today, he can still carry on a conversation while tossing yo-yos with both hands in elaborate configurations – and he can nestle a yo-yo into your shirt pocket from across the room with a flick of his wrist. **40** [ ]

When Duncan Yo-Yo went out of business, Sayegh began manufacturing yo-yos of his own patented design. He embeds six weights on each side to give them balanced mass for good momentum and links the halves with a maple-wood axle. **41** [ ] He runs the shop alone and has produced more than a million yo-yos, all of which he has sold through private shows and television appearances.

These days, the yo-yo is enjoying a resurgence in popularity and children are showing off their spinning skills in malls from Seattle to Saudi Arabia. **42** [ ] 'Fifty per cent in my shop and fifty per cent doing shows. This is nice, quiet solitude,' he says, surveying his factory domain. 'On the other side, it's hectic all over the place.'

A He may also be the only person in the world who can send two yo-yos flying off in different directions while doing the limbo.

B Sayegh finds himself living in what he calls the best of both worlds.

C The family agreed he should take it.

D It wasn't always obvious he had this skill.

E But from the beginning, he seemed to have a special knack for the spinning toy on a string.

F There, he demonstrated tricks of his own devising, with such names as 'Pistol Pete' and 'Overhand Crossfire', both of which involved two yo-yos and multiple crossings of the strings.

G His assembly line, a mesmerising contraption of bicycle parts, sewing-machine parts and industrial castoffs, allows him to single-handedly turn out one brightly coloured plastic yo-yo every forty-five seconds.

Part 7

You are going to read an article about four people who have taken up a hobby or interest. For each of the questions **43–52**, choose one of the people (**A–D**). You can choose the people more than once.

Which person

thinks their interest is becoming more popular?	43
says they never used to think they would be good at an activity?	44
says their interest requires a lot of practice?	45
says other people have liked their work?	46
says they find another activity difficult?	47
took up an activity because of a friend?	48
believes they will benefit from using different equipment?	49
compares the skills they need in one interest with the skills they need in another interest?	50
says their creative interests were interrupted by other things?	51
believes they don't fit a stereotype?	52

Developing your Talents

How a hobby or interest can transform lives.

A Colin Bartley

I'd shown an interest in art as a teenager and people often complimented me on my work and they'd tell me I should develop my talent. But as often happens with young people, creative interests are put to one side as we struggle with our academic subjects or start to take an interest in girls. Anyway, I never really did any painting for many years. I sometimes picked up a pencil and paper and did some drawing, but even then, it was only to kill time. Then a mate of mine persuaded me to go to evening classes with him. It was only a couple of hours every week but it gave me the chance to do some painting and there were no distractions. I'm really enjoying myself. I don't think I'll ever earn money from it but that's not the reason I'm doing it.

B Madeleine Curry

I started writing about five years ago when I did a short course at my local college. I then spent a year studying creative writing part-time at university. I used to be a photographer and in some ways the two activities share similarities. Writers are always observing everyday events, hoping to get an idea for their next story, much like a photographer is always looking for that great shot. Today, writers have the chance to self-publish and there's no barrier to getting your novel into the hands of readers. Because of this, more and more people are taking up writing. Some say the drawback is you don't have the satisfaction of a publisher saying your book is good enough for them to publish. But if people buy your book and the feedback is positive, that's all the praise you need.

C Grayson Collins

Believe it or not, I'm a builder by profession, not the most likely of occupations for an amateur dancer. When I was growing up, nobody in my family showed any interest in dancing and I wasn't any different. That all changed when Karen and I got married. Karen is mad about Latin dancing and we started going to classes together. I'd never done it before so we were put into separate groups but I discovered I have a talent for it. The teacher reckons I have a natural rhythm and feel for Latin dancing. That doesn't mean it comes easily. I have to do the dances again and again before I get them right but I enjoy learning new routines, especially now I'm dancing in the same group as my wife. I'm trying to get my friends to take it up as well. I know they'd enjoy themselves if they gave it a try.

D Sophie Macpherson

I started designing websites about six years ago. At first it was just a hobby but I found myself enjoying it. It's the blend of design along with the need for a mathematical eye for coding that appeals to me. It comes naturally to me, unlike the guitar, which I've been trying to play for years with little success. Over time I found myself getting quite a few jobs, and before I knew it I didn't have enough time to do both web design and my full-time job. So I left my job and set up my own business. I've recently taken out a business loan to invest in new hardware and software. Hopefully, it will enable me to take my design skills to a higher level. I think I'm lucky. I'm doing a job I enjoy, earning enough money to get by and I'm able to feed my creativity at the same time.

PAPER 2   WRITING   (1 hour 20 minutes)

Part 1

You **must** answer this question. Write your answer in an appropriate style (**140–190** words).

---

1   In your English class you have been talking about studying English.

Now your English teacher has asked you to write an essay.

Write an essay using **all** the notes and give reasons for your point of view.

Essay question

'The best way to improve your English language skills is to spend some time in an English-speaking country.'
Do you think this is true?

Notes

Write about:

1.   the benefits of being in an English-speaking country
2.   the costs involved in studying abroad
3.   your own idea

Now write your **essay**.

Part 2

You must write an answer to one of the questions **2–4**. Write your answer in an appropriate style (**140–190** words).

---

2   You see this announcement in an English-language magazine:

> **Have you got a happy memory about an event at school that you'd like to share?**
>
> Send us an article telling us what happened, when it happened and who you were with. Why was this event so memorable?
>
> The best articles will be published in the magazine.

Write your **article**.

3   You have received an email from your English-speaking friend, Chris. Read this part of the email and then write your email to Chris.

From:	Chris
Subject:	Place to stay

Hi!

It's great to hear you're coming to the UK to work. And to answer your question, yes, of course I'll be happy to help you find a place to live. Let me know what kind of place you want, how long you want it for and if you want somewhere quiet or nearer the centre.

Write your **email**.

4   You have received an email from your boss. Read this part of the email and then write your report.

From:	Greg Thomas
Subject:	Staff training

As I mentioned in our meeting, we would like to get feedback on the recent staff training day and suggestions about how future events could be improved.

Could you interview staff and write a report outlining their opinion of the training day and their suggestions for future events.

Write your **report**.

PAPER 3   LISTENING

(approx. 40 minutes,
plus 5 minutes to transfer answers)

Part 1

1 and 2

You are going to hear people talking in eight situations. For questions **1–8**, choose the correct answer (**A**, **B** or **C**).

---

1   You hear a message on an answering machine.

What does Mark want Chris to do?

A   call him

B   come to his house at 8.00

C   help him with a job

2   You hear a conversation between a father and daughter.

The daughter wants her father

A   to carry the computer.

B   to meet her in town.

C   to make an appointment.

3   You hear a lecturer making an announcement to students.

What does she tell them?

A   There are builders in the conference centre.

B   The exams have been cancelled.

C   The exams will be held in a different place.

4   You hear a radio interview with a man talking about tennis.

What can people do at the matches?

A   borrow a racket and balls

B   play for up to half an hour

C   help organise competitions

5 You hear a guide talking about an exhibition in an art gallery.

What does she say about the gallery?

A The latest exhibition is unusual for the gallery.

B It is holding an exhibition of works by various artists.

C It has exhibited work by Jason Roberts before.

6 You hear two people talking about a restaurant.

What do they say about it?

A You get a lot of food for your money.

B It only serves fish.

C It is well known for the quality of its food.

7 You hear an interview with an author about his new book.

The author says

A he intends to stop writing crime thrillers.

B he is used to doing historical research.

C he felt the need to write a historical romance.

8 You hear two students discussing a presentation.

What does the boy say about giving a presentation?

A He is pleased he doesn't have to do another one.

B It is normal to worry beforehand.

C He really enjoyed giving the presentation.

Part 2

You are going to hear a man talking about an activity he organises called orienteering. For questions **9–18**, complete the sentences. Use a word or short phrase.

ORIENTEERING

Orienteering can take place in small, managed locations like a [**9**] .

Participants have to follow each stage of the course in the [**10**] .

Courses are [**11**] coded to identify the level of difficulty.

Less challenging courses are popular with people who are accompanied by [**12**] .

The courses begin at [**13**] to make sure people work out the route on their own.

You will need a [**14**] in order to follow the course.

A whistle is important as it is sometimes hard to get a good [**15**] .

An emit card is used to [**16**] your time at each stage of the course.

You should think about wearing [**17**] to protect your legs from getting scratched.

This Saturday there is an [**18**] to an orienteering event.

Part 3

4

You are going to hear five extracts in which people talk about their reasons for doing voluntary work. For questions **19–23**, choose from the list **A–H** the reason each speaker gives. Use the letters once only. There are three letters that you do not need to use.

A   to practise a hobby

B   to increase self-confidence

Speaker 1	19

C   to deal with a local problem

Speaker 2	20

D   to help someone they know

Speaker 3	21

E   to act as a positive role model

Speaker 4	22

F   to learn practical skills

Speaker 5	23

G   to give something back

H   to make friends and feel they belong

Part 4

You are going to hear part of a radio interview with a man called Simon, who is a usability expert. For questions **24–30**, choose the correct answer (**A**, **B** or **C**).

24   How does Simon explain the meaning of usability?

   A   It considers design from different points of view.

   B   It focuses on the use of an object.

   C   It focuses on the attractiveness of an object.

25   What does Simon say about the design of the traditional potato peeler?

   A   People think it is too complicated.

   B   It is not as easy to use as modern versions.

   C   It is still popular.

26   What was the problem with the cash machine?

   A   The instructions were difficult to read.

   B   The instructions were in the wrong order.

   C   There were too many instructions.

27   What area of usability is Simon no longer involved in?

   A   household appliances

   B   software

   C   websites

28   What does Simon think is the main cause of poor web design?

   A   Planning is carried out too quickly.

   B   There are technical problems.

   C   The design is too simple.

29   What does Simon say about most companies now?

    A   They do not realise the importance of good design for websites.

    B   They appreciate the need to keep their customers happy.

    C   They offer training in usability.

30   According to Simon, what kind of people enter the field of usability?

    A   computer programmers

    B   people who have just finished university

    C   people from other areas of work

PAPER 4   SPEAKING   (14 minutes)

Candidates take the test in pairs. There are two examiners. One of the examiners will talk to you. The other examiner will listen to you. You will get marks from both examiners.

Part 1

This part of the Speaking paper lasts for about two to three minutes.

One examiner will introduce himself/herself and the other examiner. He/She will then ask you and the other candidate what your names are. After that, he/she will ask you a few basic questions. These may be about yourself, your family, your home, your daily life, your interests, etc.

Part 2

This part of the Speaking paper lasts for about four minutes.

The examiner will give you two colour photographs and ask you to describe and compare them. You will have to speak for one minute. When you have finished, the examiner will ask the other candidate to comment on your photographs. He/She will have to speak for 30 seconds.

The examiner will then give the other candidate two different photographs on the same theme and ask him/her to describe and compare them. When the other candidate has finished, the examiner will ask you to comment on the photographs. You will have to speak for 30 seconds.

The photographs for Candidate A are on page ii. The photographs for Candidate B are on page iii.

Part 3

This part of the Speaking paper lasts for about four minutes.

The examiner will give you and the other candidate instructions and some written prompts. He/She will then ask you to discuss a topic. You will have to exchange ideas with the other candidate, express and justify your opinions on the topic, agree and/or disagree, suggest, speculate and evaluate. Finally, you will have to negotiate with the other candidate to reach a decision about the topic. The prompts are on page iv.

Part 4

This part of the Speaking paper lasts for about four minutes.

The examiner will ask you and the other candidate questions related to the topic of Part 3. You will have to express and justify your opinions, agree and/or disagree and speculate about the topic.

For examples of questions the examiner might ask you in the Speaking paper, please go to page 149.

For examples of answers that would get a good mark in the Speaking paper, please go to page 165.

Test 2

PAPER 1   READING AND USE OF ENGLISH   (1 hour 15 minutes)

Part 1

For questions **1–8**, read the text below and choose which answer (**A**, **B**, **C** or **D**) best completes each gap. Here is an example (**0**).

Example:

| **0** | **A** say | **B** make | **C** do | **D** offer |

Answer:

| 0 | A ▢ | B ▆ | C ▢ | D ▢ |

Mass Marketing Fraud

Mass marketing fraud is a kind of fraud in which emails, letters, phone calls or adverts (**0**) .... false promises in order to obtain money from victims. A person does not have to benefit (**1**) .... the fraud to be guilty of the offence. As soon as they have (**2**) .... a dishonest or false statement, they have (**3**) .... a crime. Mass marketing fraudsters trick victims with false promises of cash prizes, goods or services in (**4**) .... for upfront fees. They can (**5**) .... from foreign lottery frauds to romance fraud, in which fraudsters pretend to have romantic intentions towards Internet daters to gain their trust in the (**6**) .... of obtaining money. Mass marketing fraud is becoming a more serious and complex crime. Research (**7**) .... out a few years ago showed that almost half of the UK adult population were (**8**) .... to be targeted by some kind of fraud and they estimated that UK consumers lose about £3.5 billion to fraud every year.

1 **A** from   **B** with   **C** at   **D** in

2 **A** made   **B** said   **C** done   **D** told

3 **A** carried   **B** committed   **C** completed   **D** acted

4 **A** place   **B** trade   **C** exchange   **D** turn

5 **A** reach   **B** stretch   **C** range   **D** spread

6 **A** ambition   **B** belief   **C** wish   **D** hope

7 **A** took   **B** carried   **C** made   **D** set

8 **A** likely   **B** easy   **C** available   **D** possible

Part 2

For questions **9–16**, read the text below and think of the word which best completes each gap. Use **one** word only in each gap. Here is an example (**0**).

Example:

| 0 | N | O | | | | | | | | | | | | | | | | | | | | |

Sleep may solve grammar problems

Do you know when to use 'who' and when to use 'whom'? 'Affect' and 'effect'? If you have (**0**) .... idea, open a textbook, but also (**9**) .... sure to get a good night's sleep. According to newly published research, sleep plays an important part in learning grammar. The researchers invented a new grammar (**10**) .... create sets of letter sequences or 'chunks' of letters. Students (**11**) .... told that the letter sequences were constructed according to a set of grammatical rules. They then tried to see (**12**) .... they could memorise these sequences. After that, different students waited for different lengths of time before they tried to remember the rules. Some students slept between stages and others did not. Participants (**13**) .... slept between stages performed much better (**14**) .... those who did not and were able to identify grammatical from non-grammatical letter sequences. So the next time you think you can do (**15**) .... a good night's sleep, think again. Sleep (**16**) .... just help you learn those tricky grammatical rules.

Part 3

For questions **17–24**, read the text below. Then use the word in capitals at the end of some of the lines to form a word that completes the gap in the same line. Here is an example (**0**).

Example: | **0** | A | B | I | L | I | T | Y | | | | | | | | | | | | | |

Well-being

Well-being is determined by physical and non-physical factors. The (**0**) .... of a society to produce and consume goods and services determines its standard of living. However, in the long run, even more critical is how well society manages the (**17**) .... environment and meets basic needs like food, water and clean air for the (**18**) .... of planet Earth now and in the future.

ABLE

NATURE

INHABIT

A survey carried out in 2011 showed that 73 per cent of people mentioned the environment as an important factor in well-being, only behind health, family and friends and job (**19**) .... Clearly, the negative impacts of human activity and (**20**) .... growth on the environment are an important concern. Therefore, problems such as (**21**) ...., the loss of green spaces and the (**22**) .... use of natural resources are important (**23**) .... when looking at the well-being of society. The use of land and the (**24**) .... of the countryside are also important issues that have to be addressed.

SECURE

ECONOMY

POLLUTE

EFFICIENT

CONSIDER

PROTECT

Part 4

For questions **25–30**, complete the second sentence in each pair so that it has a similar meaning to the first sentence. Use the word in capitals. **Do not change the word in capitals**. You have to use between **two** and **five** words, including the word in capitals. Here is an example (**0**).

Example:

0   The bed was so uncomfortable that we complained to the hotel manager.

   SUCH

   It .... that we complained to the hotel manager.

The gap can be completed by 'was such an uncomfortable bed' so write:

Answer: | **0** | | WAS SUCH AN UNCOMFORTABLE BED |

Write **only** the missing words **IN CAPITAL LETTERS on your answer sheet**.

---

25   Even though the weather was bad, we had a great holiday.

   SPITE

   In .... , we had a great holiday.

26   I invented an excuse because I didn't want to go to Sue's party.

   CAME

   I .... an excuse for not going to Sue's party.

27   It was three years since I had seen Mark.

   FOR

   I .... three years.

28   I didn't know there was a problem so I couldn't help.

KNOWN

Had .... the problem, I could have helped.

29   I think it would be better to have a quiet evening at home this Saturday.

SOONER

I .... a quiet evening at home this Saturday.

30   Sam probably decided to work late this evening.

MUST

Sam .... to work late this evening.

Part 5

You are going to read an extract from an adventure novel. For questions **31–36**, choose the best answer (**A**, **B**, **C** or **D**) according to the text.

I returned from the City on that May afternoon disgusted with life. I had been back in England for three months and was fed up with it. If anyone had told me a year ago that I would have been feeling like that, I would have laughed at him; but there was the fact. The weather made me feel ill, the talk of the ordinary Englishman made me sick, I couldn't get enough exercise and the entertainment in London seemed flat. 'Richard Hannay,' I kept telling myself, 'you have got into the wrong ditch, my friend, and you had better climb out.'

It made me bite my lips to think of the plans I'd made during those last years in Bulawayo. I had got my inheritance – not one of the big ones, but good enough for me – and I had figured out all kinds of ways of enjoying myself. My father had brought me out to South Africa from Scotland at the age of six and I had never been home since; so England was like an adventure to me and I counted on stopping there for the rest of my days.

But from the first I was disappointed with it. In about a week I was tired of seeing the sights and in less than a month I had had enough of restaurants and theatres and race-meetings. I had no real friend to go about with, which probably explains things. Plenty of people invited me to their houses, but they didn't seem much interested in me. A lot of ladies asked me to tea to meet schoolmasters from New Zealand and editors from Vancouver, and that was the most boring business of all. Here was I, thirty-seven years old, sound in wind and limb, with enough money to have a good time, yawning my head off all day. I had just about settled to clear out and get back to South Africa, for I was the best bored man in the United Kingdom.

That afternoon I had been worrying my brokers about investments to give my mind something to work on, and on my way home I turned into my club. I had a drink and read the evening papers. They were full of the row in the Near East, and there was an article about Karolides, the Greek Premier. I rather liked the chap. From all accounts he seemed the one big man in
line 24 the show; and he played an honest game too, which was more than could be said for most of them. I gathered that they hated him in Berlin and Vienna, but that we were going to stick by him, and one paper said that he was the only barrier between Europe and the end of the world. I remember wondering if I could get a job in those parts. It struck me that Albania was the sort of place that might keep a man from yawning.

About six o'clock I went home, dressed, dined at the Café Royal and turned into a music-hall. It was a silly show and I did not stay long. The night was fine and clear as I walked back to the flat I had hired near Portland Place. The crowd surged past me on the pavements, busy and chattering, and I envied the people for having something to do. I gave half-a-crown to a beggar because I saw him yawn; he was a fellow-sufferer. At Oxford Circus I looked up into the spring sky and I made a vow. I would give England another day to come up with something; if nothing happened, I would take the next boat for the Cape.

31 What are Hannay's feelings about London?

  A He had expected it to be more exciting.

  B He can't understand the way English people speak.

  C The people who live there are ordinary.

  D He finds it too hot.

32 What do we learn about Hannay in the second paragraph?

  A He had lived in Scotland for most of his childhood.

  B He had been planning to live in England.

  C He had spent most of his adult life in Bulawayo.

  D He was enjoying his life in South Africa.

33 What does Hannay say about his first few weeks in England?

  A There weren't enough places for him to visit.

  B He found sightseeing tiring.

  C He needed someone to explain things to him.

  D Having a friend there would have made the experience better.

34 What does Hannay suggest about 'them' when he says 'which was more than could be said for most of them'? (lines 24–25)

  A He doesn't know much about them.

  B They are less important than Karolides.

  C Karolides is more honest than most of them.

  D They are not taking the situation seriously.

35 What impression are we given of Karolides?

  A He is an important person to have around at a dangerous time.

  B The newspapers do not agree with him.

  C He is preventing Europe from expanding its influence in the world.

  D He doesn't have many supporters.

36 Why does Hannay see the beggar as 'a fellow sufferer'?

  A They both envy the people in the crowd.

  B Neither of them has a job.

  C They are both tired.

  D They are both bored.

Part 6

You are going to read an article about a scientist. Six sentences have been removed from the article. Complete the gaps (37–42) in the article with the sentences **A–G**. There is one extra sentence that you do not need to use.

The Renaissance Man:
How to become a scientist over and over again

Erez Lieberman Aiden will talk with you on any number of intellectual topics. Just don't ask him what he does. 'This is actually the most difficult question that I run into on a regular basis,' he says. 'I really don't have anything for that.'

37 [ ] Aiden is a scientist, but while most of his peers stay within a specific field – say, neuroscience or genetics – Aiden crosses them with almost casual abandon. His research has taken him across molecular biology, linguistics, physics, engineering and mathematics. He has studied the evolution of human culture through the lens of four per cent of all the books ever published. Before that, he solved the three-dimensional structure of the human genome, studied the mathematics of verbs and invented something called the iShoe, which can diagnose balance problems in elderly people. 'I guess I just view myself as a scientist,' he says.

38 [ ] Instead, Aiden is interested in problems that cross the boundaries of different disciplines. He moves about, searching for ideas that will stimulate his curiosity, extend his horizons and hopefully make a big impact. 'I don't view myself as a practitioner of a particular skill or method,' he tells me. 'I'm constantly looking at what's the most interesting problem that I could possibly work on. I really try to figure out what sort of scientist I need to be in order to solve the problem I'm interested in solving.'

39 [ ] He gravitates to problems that he knows little about. 'The reason is that most projects fail,' he says. 'If the project you know a lot about fails, you haven't gained anything. If a project you know relatively little about fails, you potentially have a bunch of new and better ideas.' And Aiden has a habit of using his failures as springboards for success.

As a child, Aiden learnt the value of being curious and well-rounded from his father, a technology entrepreneur called Aharon Lieberman. **40** [ ] 'The idea that one could support oneself by making ideas a reality is one my dad always emphasises. He gave me a lot of self-confidence. This helps, because when you suddenly change the subject in your work, all you take with you are your brains and your confidence in your own ability to figure things out.'

Aiden's approach is similar to an older era for the sciences, when people like Liebniz and Newton commanded respect in a variety of different fields. Such people are a rare breed in today's world, where the widening frontiers of scientific knowledge steer scientists into narrow specialist channels. **41** [ ] 'Thirty years ago, you didn't know what was going on in a different field and you didn't have Google. It could take you months to figure out that an idea was a good or bad one. These days, you can get a good sense of that in a matter of minutes. That's really, really huge. It makes it much easier to move from one field to another.'

The free flow of information also makes it clear how many problems there still are, enough to fill a rich career of discipline-hopping. **42** [ ] 'Now, I think, wow, we don't know anything yet.'

A Rather than specialising in any one area, Aiden takes the opposite tack.

B But Aiden senses that the balance is shifting and the connective power of the Internet plays a large part in that.

C And having expertise in a wide range of subjects has its advantages.

D It is easy to understand why.

E 'I spent many days and even summer months working with him in his factory,' says Aiden.

F 'I had this feeling out of graduate school that everything had been done,' says Aiden.

G His approach is in contrast to the standard scientific career which tends to be to find an area of interest and become increasingly knowledgeable about it.

Part 7

You are going to read an article about moving to another country. For each of the questions **43–52**, choose one of the paragraphs (**A–D**). You can choose the paragraphs more than once.

Which paragraph

comments on the difficulty of fitting into another culture?

43

states that it isn't necessarily easier to meet new people?

44

recommends getting help with accommodation?

45

suggests that our past experiences often determine how we behave?

46

says that it is sensible to move to a country for a short period to begin with?

47

suggests that there is an advantage to moving on your own?

48

gives an example of how living abroad can be cheaper?

49

argues that employment in another country can be profitable?

50

recommends maintaining financial interests at home?

51

argues that people living abroad become more open-minded?

52

A New Life Abroad

Many of us dream of starting a new life abroad. But is the reality as good as the dream?

A The promise of a better quality of life is often quoted as the main reason for moving abroad. The possibility of making new friends, of spending more time with the family and having more opportunities for leisure activities are examples of how people believe this may be achieved. However, the hope of a better life is often difficult to realise. When you take off to another country, you take your emotional baggage with you. Why should it be easier to make friends in a strange culture? Why should life in another country offer you the freedom to spend more time with your family? Would you really become a more active person simply by living abroad? Advice to those with this ambition is to be clear what you want and why moving abroad is the answer.

B The need to find work is a major reason for moving to another country. Taking up a position abroad can offer exciting challenges and result in better working conditions and remuneration. If you class yourself as a potential occupational migrant, the advice is to secure a position before you move, making sure contracts have been read, agreed and signed on both sides. Experts also recommend testing the water first by taking up seasonal work such as a summer job or a short-term contract to get a feel for the country and the experience of working abroad. It can also be useful if your employer can find you somewhere to live, or is willing to subsidise your housing costs, even on a temporary basis.

C Students are another group for whom the idea of spending time abroad is appealing. As entry into university becomes more competitive, students are more willing to consider doing a course in another country. Many universities target international students; indeed many of them depend on the income such students bring in. Courses abroad could be more suited to your interests. What is more, living abroad and gaining experience of another culture can make you more valuable to future employers. Opportunities in both work and your social life open up dramatically as your circle of contacts grows. Relocating on your own, without friends and family, will force you to get out and meet new people. And of course, it is generally accepted that people who live abroad become more tolerant and appreciative of other cultures. Advice to anyone looking into this option but wary of doing an entire degree abroad is to consider a course that offers one year abroad as part of the overall degree.

D Enjoying retirement is another motivation for moving abroad. The idea of spending your later years somewhere warm and sunny is popular with many people from colder climates and a lifetime of savings can often last longer if you move to a country with a lower standard of living. Decisions on where to go are often made on the basis of a favourite summer holiday destination. However, does a two-week holiday really give you a clear idea of the consequences of uprooting and relocating abroad? Many people returning home after a failed attempt at emigration cite missing friends and family as a major cause of unhappiness. And of course, healthcare becomes a major cause for concern for senior citizens; not having a clear idea of what you are entitled to can also lead to disappointment. Experts advise anyone thinking of moving abroad to avoid selling their homes. They recommend renting properties out instead so that there is something to return to should things go wrong.

PAPER 2   WRITING   (1 hour 20 minutes)

Part 1

You **must** answer this question. Write your answer in an appropriate style (**140–190** words).

___

1   In your English class you have been talking about employment.

Now your English teacher has asked you to write an essay.

Write an essay using **all** the notes and give reasons for your point of view.

HOMEWORK

Essay title

'Younger people should be given priority over older people when applying for jobs.'
Do you agree?

Notes

Write about:

1. *the importance of younger people getting their first job*
2. *the wider experience older people have*
3. *your own idea*

Now write your **essay**.

Part 2

You must write an answer to one of the questions **2–4**. Write your answer in an appropriate style (**140–190** words).

2   You see this announcement in an international student magazine:

> **Is there a popular festival that takes place in your country?**
> **Is it something our readers would enjoy reading about?**
>
> You are invited to send in a review of a local or national festival you know about.
> The best submissions will be included in next month's magazine.

Write your **review**.

3   You have received an email from an English-speaking friend, Emma. Read this part of the email and then write your email to Emma.

From:	Emma
Subject:	Party Invitation

Many thank for inviting me to your party! Yes, I'd love to come!

I've never been to your home so could you tell me the best way to get there? I'll be arriving at the airport so directions from there would be great. What's the weather like at the moment? I'm wondering if I need to bring warm clothes.

Write your **email**.

4   Your English teacher has asked you to write about the shopping facilities in your area. You should say what people like about the facilities and what could be done to improve them.

Carry out a survey of local people and write a report on your findings.

Write your **report**.

PAPER 3   LISTENING

(approx. 40 minutes,
plus 5 minutes to transfer answers)

Part 1

You are going to hear people talking in eight situations. For questions **1–8**, choose the correct answer (**A**, **B** or **C**).

---

1 You hear a conversation between a man and a woman at a party.

Where does the man live?

A Manchester

B London

C Birmingham

2 You hear an interview on the radio with a cyclist.

Which country has she recently cycled through?

A France

B Spain

C Switzerland

3 You hear a guide talking to visitors in an art gallery.

Why is the main hall closed?

A The paintings are being moved.

B The room is being decorated.

C The floor has been damaged.

4 You hear a man talking to a police officer.

What is the man's problem?

A He is looking for his wife.

B He can't get into his car.

C He can't find his car.

5   You hear a customer talking to a waiter in a café.

What does she order?

A   a bowl of soup

B   a sandwich

C   a cream cake

6   You hear a student leaving a message on an answering machine.

He is

A   confident about doing his exams.

B   pleased he has an early morning exam.

C   unsure about one of the topics.

7   You hear a woman called Judy talking on the phone to her friend Martin.

What does she want?

A   a lift to a party

B   to ask if he wants to share a taxi

C   to go to his house

8   You hear a footballer talking about his career.

What is he most proud of?

A   winning an award for being the best player

B   holding a record for the number of games played

C   never having received a yellow card

Part 2

7

You are going to hear a man talking about courses in Internet security.
For questions **9–18**, complete the sentences. Use a word or short phrase.

Dealing with Internet Security

The Internet safety sessions will take place in the [_____ **9**].

When creating passwords, some people use their [_____ **10**]
or even 'password'.

Criminals often send emails pretending to be from a well-known
[_____ **11**].

People should watch out for emails that say you have recently
[_____ **12**] and that you need to check the details are correct.

One session will give advice about using [_____ **13**] safely,
both in the home and outside it.

People need to be careful about sharing personal information with others when using
[_____ **14**].

Users should get to know the [_____ **15**] on the websites
they use.

Sharing personal information like photos is particularly important with regards to
[_____ **16**].

The final session will look at how to protect the [_____ **17**]
files on your computer.

Three of the speaker's computers broke down in a [_____ **18**].

Part 3

You are going to hear five extracts in which people talk about a journey they have made. For questions **19–23**, choose from the list **A–H** the reason each speaker gives for enjoying the journey. Use the letters once only. There are three letters that you do not need to use.

A   the kindness of other people

B   getting to their destination quickly

Speaker 1	19

C   getting to know local people

Speaker 2	20

D   the safety of the journey

Speaker 3	21

E   visiting out-of-the-way places

Speaker 4	22

F   using the Internet to plan their journey

Speaker 5	23

G   being able to read while travelling

H   the beautiful scenery

Part 4

You are going to hear part of a radio interview with a woman called Claire, who does mountain running. For questions **24–30**, choose the correct answer (**A**, **B** or **C**).

24   What does Claire say about mountain running?

    A   The name is a little misleading.

    B   It is worse than you can imagine.

    C   It is exhausting and time-consuming.

25   People who live in the city

    A   prefer running in the Lake District and the Highlands of Scotland.

    B   must be able to drive to get to the countryside.

    C   can probably find a mountain running club near their home.

26   Currently, most mountain running races

    A   are held at fairs or during festivals.

    B   are independent sporting events.

    C   have participants from many countries.

27   The Dragon's Back race

    A   is open to anyone who wants to sign up.

    B   is not as challenging as some other courses.

    C   only allows certain people to do the run.

28   What does Claire say about participating in races?

    A   People shouldn't feel obliged to do them.

    B   They are only suitable for people who are very fit.

    C   They help you to stay motivated.

29   What does Claire say about road running?

    A   Runners don't have the chance to appreciate nature.

    B   It is harder than mountain running.

    C   Runners are more likely to suffer certain injuries.

30   According to Claire, experienced road runners

    A   find the uneven surface of mountain running a challenge.

    B   can adapt to mountain running quickly.

    C   will be able to run faster than they think.

PAPER 4　　SPEAKING　　　　　　　　(14 minutes)

Candidates take the test in pairs. There are two examiners. One of the examiners will talk to you. The other examiner will listen to you. You will get marks from both examiners.

Part 1

This part of the Speaking paper lasts for about two to three minutes.

One examiner will introduce himself/herself and the other examiner. He/She will then ask you and the other candidate what your names are. After that, he/she will ask you a few basic questions. These may be about yourself, your family, your home, your daily life, your interests, etc.

Part 2

This part of the Speaking paper lasts for about four minutes.

The examiner will give you two colour photographs and ask you to describe and compare them. You will have to speak for one minute. When you have finished, the examiner will ask the other candidate to comment on your photographs. He/She will have to speak for 30 seconds.

The examiner will then give the other candidate two different photographs on the same theme and ask him/her to describe and compare them. When the other candidate has finished, the examiner will ask you to comment on the photographs. You will have to speak for 30 seconds.

The photographs for Candidate A are on page vi. The photographs for Candidate B are on page vii.

Part 3

This part of the Speaking paper lasts for about four minutes.

The examiner will give you and the other candidate instructions and some written prompts. He/She will then ask you to discuss a topic. You will have to exchange ideas with the other candidate, express and justify your opinions on the topic, agree and/or disagree, suggest, speculate and evaluate. Finally, you will have to negotiate with the other candidate to reach a decision about the topic. The prompts are on page viii.

Part 4

This part of the Speaking paper lasts for about four minutes.

The examiner will ask you and the other candidate questions related to the topic of Part 3. You will have to express and justify your opinions, agree and/or disagree and speculate about the topic.

For examples of questions the examiner might ask you in the Speaking paper, please go to page 153.

For examples of answers that would get a good mark in the Speaking paper, please go to page 168.

Test 3

PAPER 1   READING AND USE OF ENGLISH   (1 hour 15 minutes)

Part 1

For questions **1–8**, read the text below and choose which answer (**A**, **B**, **C** or **D**) best completes each gap. Here is an example (**0**).

Example:

0   **A** turn   **B** change   **C** switch   **D** move

Answer:
0	A	B	C	D
	▬			

Transport Patterns

The twentieth century saw dramatic changes in how the British travel. By the (**0**) .... of the century, the rail network was largely in (**1**) .... Horse-drawn transport ruled the roads and cars were not a (**2**) .... sight. However, in the 1920s the way in which people travelled across the country changed. Motorised buses and mass-produced cars (**3**) .... horse-drawn transport. New roads were built to (**4**) .... with the growing number of motorised vehicles, while the rail network started to see a decline in passenger numbers. Commercial air flights also (**5**) .... in popularity during the second half of the last century. But the situation is continuing to change. Travel by car is still the dominant form of travel in the twenty-first century but bus and rail travel has begun to increase whereas air travel shows (**6**) .... of slowing down, partly because people have started to reflect (**7**) .... the ways they travel and their (**8**) .... on our environment.

1   **A** post   **B** position   **C** place   **D** plant

2   **A** general   **B** regular   **C** routine   **D** common

3   **A** replaced   **B** changed   **C** reformed   **D** altered

4   **A** deal   **B** handle   **C** manage   **D** attend

5   **A** widened   **B** stretched   **C** spread   **D** grew

6   **A** hints   **B** signs   **C** marks   **D** clues

7   **A** in   **B** of   **C** about   **D** on

8   **A** product   **B** reaction   **C** effect   **D** result

Part 2

For questions **9–16**, read the text below and think of the word which best completes each gap. Use **one** word only in each gap. Here is an example (**0**).

Example: | **0** | T | O | | | | | | | | | | | | | | | | | | | |

Where might a degree take you?

A university degree can lead (**0**) .... a well-defined career path, and each year students make choices that will have an impact on their employment prospects. However, (**9**) .... you are looking into the courses available, bear in mind that your choice need not necessarily restrict your future career options.

Research carried (**10**) .... in London examined how the choice of degree subject influences a graduate's occupation and the sector of the economy in which they take up employment. Researchers asked people about their occupations and (**11**) .... undergraduate degree they studied for. Their findings showed (**12**) .... although people with architecture or engineering as a first degree work mainly (**13**) .... architects or engineers, other undergraduate degrees lead to a variety of possible occupations. For example, London residents (**14**) .... have studied business and administrative studies (**15**) .... employed in most sectors of the London economy, and less (**16**) .... one-fifth of those who studied creative arts and design worked in the arts, entertainment and recreation sectors.

Part 3

For questions **17–24**, read the text below. Then use the word in capitals at the end of some of the lines to form a word that completes the gap in the same line. Here is an example (**0**).

Example: | 0 | U | P | L | O | A | D | E | D | | | | | | | | | | | |

The Impact of the Internet

On 6 August 1991 Sir Tim Berners-Lee (**0**) .... the first ever website to the Internet. Since then the World Wide Web has changed the way we work, find (**17**) ...., learn, shop and even make friends. The World Wide Web is also contributing to the (**18**) .... of new vocabulary, with 'to google' becoming a recognisable verb. According to research, 2.4 billion people were online by the end of 2012, which is equal to one third of the world's (**19**) ....

LOAD

EMPLOY

CREATE

POPULATE

The World Wide Web empowers individuals by enabling them to access or post (**20**) .... online, removing control of information from governments and the media. It has also been suggested that the Internet could change how government works, improving (**21**) ...., increasing choice and encouraging greater (**22**) .... On the other hand, serious concerns have been raised over (**23**) .... and security as personal information is captured and manipulated online. There are also concerns that some people are at a (**24**) .... because they have no access to the Internet.

KNOW

TRANSPARENT

RESPONSIBLE

PRIVATE

ADVANTAGE

Part 4

For questions **25–30**, complete the second sentence in each pair so that it has a similar meaning to the first sentence. Use the word in capitals. **Do not change the word in capitals**. You have to use between **two** and **five** words, including the word in capitals. Here is an example (**0**).

Example:

0   The teacher said that Kevin had broken the window.

ACCUSED

Kevin .... the window.

The gap can be completed by the words 'was accused of breaking' so you write:

Answer: | **0** | | WAS ACCUSED OF BREAKING |

Write **only** the missing words **IN CAPITAL LETTERS on the separate answer sheet**.

---

25   John doesn't want to go out so it is a waste of time asking him.

POINT

There .... asking John as he doesn't want to go out.

26   Commuters have been delayed by serious traffic jams.

UP

Commuters .... by serious traffic jams.

27   I know she was angry but Sarah shouldn't have lost her temper.

NEED

I know she was angry but there .... Sarah to lose her temper.

28   I think Tony should take a day off and call the doctor.

ASK

If ...., Tony should take a day off and call the doctor.

29   I didn't want to go because I thought it was a bad idea.

OBJECTED

I .... because I thought it was a bad idea.

30   Karen knew nothing about the surprise party they had organised.

IDEA

Karen .... that they had organised a surprise party.

Part 5

You are going to read an extract from a short story. For questions **31–36**, choose the best answer (**A, B, C** or **D**) according to the text.

Room Nineteen at the Montrose Club

The taxi driver refused to stop outside the entrance. 'Parking restrictions. Traffic wardens are all over the place round here.' Thinking of his tip perhaps, he got out of the taxi and came round to open the door, offering his passenger a strong arm to grip. Once Miss Sharpe was safely on the pavement, he reached into the back seat for her luggage. In the short walk she battled against an April wind that nearly whipped her hat off her head. The entrance door blew shut as soon as she was inside. Moments later the taxi driver pushed it open again and dropped her bags on to the floor. She gave him a generous tip but that didn't stop him looking at the notes as though he expected her to add a couple more.

She looked around the hotel lobby. Someone had been painting the smoke-yellowed ceiling white and must have run out of paint, because they had left a corner unfinished. It was only a small area, so she decided not to mention it straight away. During her spell in hospital she had dreamt of her return to the Montrose Club: she had pictured Fats on reception, his mouth breaking into a huge grin at the sight of her before he cried, 'Miss Sharpe, where have you been!' In another dream, the management had organised a welcoming party ('afternoon tea for our favourite resident') in the Clarendon Lounge.

Lying in the hospital bed, she had practised the story of her absence so often that she was word perfect, and if a little embellishment had crept into the script with each run-through, that was only normal. 'Accident with a thief. I say accident, but his intentions were entirely deliberate. Grabbed my bag. Didn't realise I always wear the strap looped around my finger. Wrenched it out of its socket. Had to be reset. Twice.' A pause and then: 'The worst thing was that it happened in broad daylight in the middle of Oxford Street.' She remembered, or thought she remembered, sitting on the ground with one leg bent painfully underneath her. People rushed past, taking a diversion around her as if she were a roundabout.

The reception desk was unattended. She banged the bell with her good hand and Fats, so called because of his narrow frame and love of jazz piano, appeared from the back room. He worked alternate days at the Montrose Club from eight until six o'clock, followed by a four-hour shift at a public house around the corner. 'Good afternoon, Fats. I hope my room is ready.'

Fats rented a flat in Brixton and each week he sent money to his mother in Lagos. Once, against club rules, she tried to tip him privately. He had stared at the twenty-pound note held in his open palm and then pointed to the money box labelled 'Staff Fund'. All staff were obliged to share gratuities equally. Her intention had never been to test his character. Nevertheless, she was pleased at this proof of his honesty. He looked thinner than ever.

'Just one moment, Miss Sharpe. Your room, I'm afraid ...'

'Oh, surely not!'

'We weren't sure when to expect you back. If you could just manage for two nights –'

'But room nineteen is my room. You know that.'

'It will be free the day after tomorrow. On my life, Miss Sharpe. If anyone else wants room nineteen they'll have to get past me first.' He struck a pose like a warrior before collapsing into laughter and placing the key to room twenty-three in her hand.

31   In the first paragraph, it appears that the taxi driver

   A   has seen a traffic warden.

   B   is satisfied with how much he is paid.

   C   holds the hotel door open for Miss Sharpe.

   D   carries Miss Sharpe's luggage.

32   What do we learn about Miss Sharpe in the second paragraph?

   A   She is expecting a warm welcome from the hotel.

   B   The Montrose Club is her dream hotel.

   C   She is a popular guest at the hotel.

   D   She doesn't like the new colour the ceiling has been painted.

33   When meeting the hotel staff, Miss Sharpe

   A   wants to give a true account of what happened to her.

   B   knows she will be emotional when explaining what happened to her.

   C   wants to show she has a good memory of what happened to her.

   D   knows what she is going to say.

34   The receptionist

   A   has an office in the back room.

   B   is overweight.

   C   works every other day at the hotel.

   D   is playing the piano.

35   What do we learn about Miss Sharpe's view of Fats?

   A   She is worried about his health.

   B   She thinks he is honest.

   C   She isn't sure if he can be trusted.

   D   He likes to break the rules of the hotel.

36   Room nineteen

   A   is reserved by Miss Sharpe.

   B   is being used by the hotel management.

   C   is only available for two nights.

   D   is currently unavailable.

Part 6

You are going to read an article about being active on vacation. Six sentences have been removed from the article. Complete the gaps (**37–42**) in the article with the sentences **A–G**. There is one extra sentence that you do not need to use.

Physically Active Vacations: Why They Are Good For You

In the autumn of 2009 my wife Daun and I went on a cycling trip through the Rocky Mountains. We had been invited to a wedding in Canmore, Alberta one weekend, and another in Chase, British Columbia the following weekend. The two cities are roughly 300 miles apart, and since we had a full week to make the trip, we decided to do it on our road bikes. **37** Canmore is about one mile above sea level, while Chase is less than a quarter-mile above sea level, and we had plenty of time, so we were able to take our time and enjoy our ride.

People often talk about how difficult it is to maintain a healthy lifestyle while on vacation. **38** It's fun for a day or two, but you wind up feeling awful and need a vacation to detoxify from your vacation. So I started to question why, out of all the things one could choose to do for a vacation, people would choose to put themselves in an environment where they will have no choice but to eat unhealthy food and perform very little physical activity – two things that are almost guaranteed to make them feel awful.

I thought a lot about this issue on my trip and I realised that instead of taking vacations that pigeon-hole us into unhealthy behaviours, we would all be better off taking vacations that force us to engage in healthy behaviours. Things like hiking, skiing, cycling and canoeing are not only healthy, but they're cheap! **39** We took our first cycling vacation in 2008, when we set up shop in a small Bed and Breakfast in Picton, Ontario. Each day we would do a different short ride from our B&B. It cost us almost nothing, and it was literally the best vacation I've ever had. And after a few days of exercising and eating well, we came home feeling completely re-energised.

Not surprisingly, limited evidence supports the idea that healthy vacations leave you feeling better than those characterised by gluttony and sloth. For example, Gerhard Strauss-Blasche and colleagues examined the links between vacation environment and recuperation in a study published in the *Journal of Travel Medicine*. **40** Post-vacation 'recuperation' was assessed by quantifying how closely subjects agreed with the statement 'In comparison to the two weeks before vacation, I now feel mentally fitter, feel more balanced and relaxed, can concentrate better during work, feel physically fitter, do my work more easily, am in a better mood and feel more recuperated'.

So what did the authors find? Physical activity during the trip was positively associated with post-vacation recuperation scores. **41** In fact, healthy behaviours including physical activity and adequate sleep accounted for seven per cent of the post-vacation recuperation.

42 In fact, I wouldn't take this study too seriously. But I don't think it's surprising that people who engage in healthy behaviours during a vacation might feel better upon their return. So instead of looking at your vacation as a potential stumbling block to your healthy lifestyle, why not look at it as a chance to improve your healthy behaviours?

A The study included 191 German males and females, who filled out questionnaires within two weeks of returning from a short vacation.

B A cruise ship is the perfect example – too much food and too little exercise.

C Not surprisingly, these figures have resulted in a huge change in attitudes.

D Crossing the Rockies on a bike sounds pretty intense, and it certainly wasn't easy, but luckily most of the trip was downhill.

E In other words, the more physically active people were during their vacation, the more likely they were to feel recuperated upon their return.

F Now of course this is only one study, and it only used questionnaire data, which is less than ideal.

G That's why Daun and I first started taking cycling vacations – we couldn't afford to do much else!

Part 7

You are going to read an article about four people's most treasured possessions. For each of the questions **43–52**, choose one of the people (**A–D**). You can choose the people more than once.

_____

Which person

admits they are acting out of character? | 43 |

enjoys looking at their possession? | 44 |

believes their luck might change if they no longer had their possession? | 45 |

has several items that they have an emotional attachment to? | 46 |

intends to pass things on to their child/children? | 47 |

is planning to make a change to their house? | 48 |

describes something that makes them feel unhappy? | 49 |

imagines their possession being used in the past? | 50 |

thinks their possession could be worth a lot of money? | 51 |

says their possession attracts attention? | 52 |

Treasured Possessions

Most of us have possessions that we treasure. Four people talk to us about theirs.

A The plant has been in the family for years. It was a cutting taken from a plant at my parents' house and they'd had theirs since I was a child, so that's at least 50 years. It's a money tree and it's supposed to be an indicator of the owner's financial condition. If the plant is unhealthy, it means your finances are also suffering. I hate to think what would happen if mine died! It's so big that it was difficult finding somewhere to put it. It's in the kitchen at the moment but we're going to have the room re-designed so we need to find a new home for it. It's not a particularly attractive plant but because of its size, everyone who visits comments on it. The children aren't fond of it so I don't think we'll be handing it down to them. I don't want to risk ending up in poverty if I throw it out so we'll have to wait and see.

B One of the things my father left me was a knife. He was in the navy during the war and all recruits were issued with one of these knives. He called it a deep sea diving knife and whenever he showed it to me as a child, I imagined him diving to great depths in a diving suit with this knife in his belt. It never occurred to me that since my father wasn't a great swimmer he probably wouldn't have dived at all. Since his death I've kept it locked away and I've also done some research to find out more about it. Apparently, it's collectible and people are prepared to pay a lot for certain models. Whenever I look at it, I have fond memories of my father and I still like to think he put it to good use all those years ago.

C I've got things that are important to me – my computer and objects that have sentimental value, like the photos of my children and my wedding ring. But my most treasured possessions are the memories I have of my children growing up. They still live with us and we have wonderful times together so the memories are constantly being added to. Memories of holidays, family parties and get-togethers are particularly happy. Of course, there were also events that I wish hadn't happened, such as the accidents they had as small children. These still upset me but all in all, my memories are of happy times. Some of these occasions were caught on video or in photos. If we lost them, I'd be upset but it's the memories themselves I cherish most.

D I'm not sentimental and don't usually hang on to things so I suppose it's surprising that the possessions that stand out are the letters I have from my son when he was younger. He used to travel a lot during his twenties and would send me wonderful letters telling me where he was and what he was doing. Some of them were quite exciting – one described a train journey on which he shared a carriage with some coffee smugglers. Other letters were more disturbing, such as one in which he described being robbed. You can imagine how concerned I was reading it at the time but now it's just a reminder of an adventure. Then there's the letter in which he explained he'd met a wonderful girl. That girl eventually became his wife and my daughter-in-law. I know my son wants me to keep these letters and eventually I'll give them to him.

PAPER 2   WRITING

(1 hour 20 minutes)

Part 1

You **must** answer this question. Write your answer in an appropriate style (**140–190** words).

1   In your English class you have been talking about food.

Now your English teacher has asked you to write an essay.

Write an essay using **all** the notes and give reasons for your point of view.

Essay question

'The threat to our health from processed food is so serious that governments must take steps to make sure we eat more healthily.' Do you think this is correct?

Notes

Write about:

1. *how governments could regulate the food industry*
2. *the importance of personal choice*
3. *your own idea*

Now write your **essay**.

Part 2

You must write an answer to one of the questions **2–4**. Write your answer in an appropriate style (**140–190** words).

---

2   Your English teacher has asked you to write about crime in your local area. You should say what people think are the main problems and what could be done to improve the situation. Carry out a survey of local people and write a report on your findings.

Write your **report**.

3   You have received an email from an English-speaking friend, Anna. Read the email and then write your email to Anna.

From: Anna
Subject: College project

Hi Eva,

I hope you and your family are well. I have a favour to ask. We're doing a project at school about how teenagers spend their weekends in other countries. Where do people go where you live? Are there any popular leisure activities?

All the best,
Anna

Write your **email**.

4   You see this announcement on an English-language website:

Holiday of a Lifetime!

Where would you like to go if you could take a holiday anywhere in the world? Who would you go with? What would you do during the holiday?

Write us an article answering these questions. We will publish the best articles on our website.

Write your **article**.

PAPER 3   LISTENING

(approx. 40 minutes,
plus 5 minutes to transfer answers)

Part 1

10

You are going to hear people talking in eight situations. For questions **1–8**, choose the best answer (**A**, **B** or **C**).

---

1   You hear two people talking about a film they have just seen.

Why didn't the woman enjoy herself?

A   The film was too long.

B   The seats were uncomfortable.

C   The people around them were talking.

2   You hear a woman talking on the radio about a business she runs.

What is she planning to do?

A   start a company

B   employ more people

C   launch a new product

3   You hear a message on an answering machine.

When does the meeting start?

A   2.30

B   3.00

C   5.00

4   You hear a man and a woman talking about the man's car.

Why can't the man use his car at the moment?

A   it isn't working

B   he doesn't have it

C   it isn't insured

5   You hear a message from a school secretary on an answering machine.

What does the school want the parents to do?

A   collect their child now

B   give their child some sun cream

C   supply a packed lunch

6   You hear a customer talking to a shop assistant.

What does the customer decide to do?

A   return to the shop later

B   buy the suit

C   have the suit altered

7   You hear a shopkeeper being interviewed on the radio.

He is unhappy because

A   the bus service is very poor.

B   there isn't enough parking space.

C   some shopkeepers are causing problems.

8   You hear an employee talking to her boss.

What does she want?

A   to be able to use the company Intranet

B   a replacement computer

C   to be transferred to a different job

Part 2

11

You are going to hear a college manager telling new members of staff about training opportunities. For questions **9–18**, complete the sentences. Use a word or short phrase.

College Staff Training

The staff training programme at the college has featured in national

<u>   **9** </u>.

The opportunity for <u>   **10** </u> within the college is improved

when a person updates their skills.

The most important reason for staff development is to provide students with

<u>   **11** </u>.

Team meetings are held three times a year, during the final week of each

<u>   **12** </u>.

The college will pay the costs of training requirements

<u>   **13** </u>.

People attending training courses must fill in a <u>   **14** </u>

which they must share with their colleagues.

The college will remain closed on <u>   **15** </u>

and there are no classes for students.

Food provided in the <u>   **16** </u> on college training days is free.

Part of an 'away day' could be spent doing <u>   **17** </u>

activities like ice skating, climbing or orienteering.

People holding an 'away day' at their home can claim £100 towards

<u>   **18** </u> costs.

Part 3

12

You are going to hear five extracts in which people talk about money.
For questions **19–23**, choose from the list **A–H** the attitude each speaker has towards money. Use the letters once only. There are three letters that you do not need to use.

A   They wouldn't change if they were rich.

B   They would feel uncomfortable being rich.

Speaker 1	19

C   They would be able to travel if they were rich.

Speaker 2	20

D   They would hate to be in debt.

Speaker 3	21

E   They would have a greater sense of security if they were rich.

Speaker 4	22

F   They would like to leave their children money.

Speaker 5	23

G   They would like to go on a spending spree.

H   They would give away most of the money.

Part 4

13

You are going to hear part of a radio interview with a woman called Molly, who flies commercial aeroplanes. For questions **24–30**, choose the correct answer (**A**, **B** or **C**).

---

24 What does Molly say about her decision to become a pilot?

    A As a child she couldn't stop talking about it.

    B It wasn't her first career ambition.

    C It was a surprising choice.

25 Molly's parents

    A explained that being a pilot was a male-dominated profession.

    B were supportive about her choice of career.

    C would have preferred other career options for their daughter.

26 What did Molly have to do in order to get her private pilot's licence?

    A get a university degree

    B do a job she didn't really enjoy

    C study for 150 hours

27 What does Molly say about getting a full commercial pilot's licence?

    A You don't need to do theory tests.

    B It costs too much money for most people.

    C You can't get one until you complete a lot of other training.

28 What does Molly say about being first officer?

    A The captain decides when she can fly the plane.

    B She gets the chance to take off occasionally.

    C She shares the job of flying the plane with the captain.

29   What is the advantage of being a senior first officer?

    A   You can train other people to fly.

    B   There are fewer restrictions on where you can land.

    C   You can fly to destinations with better weather.

30   What does Molly say about choosing a career as a pilot?

    A   You shouldn't try to become one unless you are serious about flying.

    B   It is an exciting, well-paid job.

    C   People don't realise how much money it costs to become one.

PAPER 4   SPEAKING   (14 minutes)

Candidates take the test in pairs. There are two examiners. One of the examiners will talk to you. The other examiner will listen to you. You will get marks from both examiners.

Part 1

This part of the Speaking paper lasts for about two to three minutes.

One examiner will introduce himself/herself and the other examiner. He/She will then ask you and the other candidate what your names are. After that, he/she will ask you a few basic questions. These may be about yourself, your family, your home, your daily life, your interests, etc.

Part 2

This part of the Speaking paper lasts for about four minutes.

The examiner will give you two colour photographs and ask you to describe and compare them. You will have to speak for one minute. When you have finished, the examiner will ask the other candidate to comment on your photographs. He/She will have to speak for 30 seconds.

The examiner will then give the other candidate two different photographs on the same theme and ask him/her to describe and compare them. When the other candidate has finished, the examiner will ask you to comment on the photographs. You will have to speak for 30 seconds.

The photographs for Candidate A are on page x. The photographs for Candidate B are on page xi.

Part 3

This part of the Speaking paper lasts for about four minutes.

The examiner will give you and the other candidate instructions and some written prompts. He/She will then ask you to discuss a topic. You will have to exchange ideas with the other candidate, express and justify your opinions on the topic, agree and/or disagree, suggest, speculate and evaluate. Finally, you will have to negotiate with the other candidate to reach a decision about the topic. The prompts are on page xii.

Part 4

This part of the Speaking paper lasts for about four minutes.

The examiner will ask you and the other candidate questions related to the topic of Part 3. You will have to express and justify your opinions, agree and/or disagree and speculate about the topic.

For examples of questions the examiner might ask you in the Speaking paper, please go to page 157.

For examples of answers that would get a good mark in the Speaking paper, please go to page 172.

Test 4

PAPER 1   READING AND USE OF ENGLISH   (1 hour 15 minutes)

Part 1

For questions **1–8**, read the text below and choose which answer (**A, B, C** or **D**) best completes each gap. Here is an example (**0**).

Example:

0   **A** makes   **B** plays   **C** turns   **D** comes

Answer: | **0** | **A** ☐ | **B** ☐ | **C** ▬ | **D** ☐ |

A Long-standing Relationship

According to a recent study, it (**0**) .... out that thousands of years ago humans loved to share food with, play with and dress up their pet dogs, (**1**) .... as we do today. The study investigated the (**2**) .... of the ancient human-dog relationship by analysing specimens from Siberia. It (**3**) .... to light that the dogs buried around 7,000–8,000 years ago were only found at burial sites shared with humans. Dogs were buried in resting positions or immediately next to humans, and their (**4**) .... often included various items seemingly (**5**) .... for the dogs. One dog (**6**) .... particular had a necklace made of red deer teeth around its neck and deer remains by its side, and another was buried with what (**7**) .... to be a pebble or toy in its mouth. The researchers were also able to determine similarities in human and dog diets. The nature of the burials and the similarities in diet (**8**) .... to an intimate and personal relationship between humans and their dogs.

1 **A** much   **B** more   **C** like   **D** similar

2 **A** pattern   **B** style   **C** form   **D** nature

3 **A** came   **B** moved   **C** grew   **D** set

4 **A** ditches   **B** graves   **C** shrines   **D** trenches

5 **A** planned   **B** suited   **C** meant   **D** aimed

6 **A** at   **B** on   **C** in   **D** for

7 **A** emerged   **B** looked   **C** showed   **D** appeared

8 **A** hint   **B** point   **C** indicate   **D** tend

Part 2

For questions **9–16**, read the text below and think of the word which best completes each gap. Use **one** word only in each gap. Here is an example (**0**).

Example:

0	O	F																		

Manly health

According to a recent survey, males (**0**) .... all ages are more likely to practise behaviours linked to higher mortality (**9**) .... females. They are also less likely to practise protective behaviours. Indeed, it is a sad fact that in modern-day society (**10**) .... is a belief that being healthy is not manly! Apparently, caring about your body, (**11**) .... you eat and how you live, makes you less of a man. If I want to be 'manly', I need to ignore my stresses and emotions. Even seeing my doctor is not regarded (**12**) .... a masculine thing to do. To be manly, I have to ignore what my doctor tells me, and worst of (**13**) ...., I am only really manly (**14**) .... I don't actually care! Why is (**15**) .... that caring about my health, protecting my skin from the sun, avoiding sugary and fatty foods and sharing my stresses is something that should only (**16**) .... done by women? Being healthy, whether you are a man or woman, should be encouraged, celebrated and congratulated.

Part 3

For questions **17–24**, read the text below. Then use the word in capitals at the end of some of the lines to form a word that completes the gap in the same line. Here is an example (**0**).

Example: | 0 | I | N | D | U | S | T | R | I | A | L | | | | | | | | | | |

Global warming: a growing concern

Climate change refers to the long-term change in the patterns of
average weather, temperature, wind and rainfall. Before the (**0**) .... **INDUSTRY**
revolution, climate was influenced entirely by natural events and
processes, for example, major (**17**) .... eruptions, tropical storms **VOLCANO**
and (**18**) ....in ocean currents. Over the last 100 years, when human **VARY**
(**19**) .... has added to natural factors, the Earth has warmed by **ACTIVE**
0.7°C, and since the 1970s by 0.4°C. In 2007 an inter-governmental
report stated that our (**20**) .... in the warming of the climate could **INVOLVE**
no longer be doubted. A panel came to the (**21**) ....that greenhouse **CONCLUDE**
gas emissions will continue to increase unless there are (**22**) .... **EFFECT**
international efforts to reverse the trend. On current (**23**) ...., this **PROJECT**
could result in the climate warming by between 1.7°C and 4.0°C by
2100. Globally, this will mean extreme weather, and in some parts of
the world this will cause food (**24**) .... and disease. **SHORT**

Part 4

For questions **25–30**, complete the second sentence in each pair so that it has a similar meaning to the first sentence. Use the word in capitals. **Do not change the word in capitals**. You have to use between **two** and **five** words, including the word in capitals. Here is an example (**0**).

Example:

0   Why didn't you tell me you were feeling ill?

   SHOULD

   You .... me you were feeling ill.

The gap can be completed by 'should have told' so write:

Answer: | **0** | SHOULD HAVE TOLD |

Write **only** the missing words **IN CAPITAL LETTERS on your answer sheet.**

_____

25   The children couldn't play outside because it was raining.

   POSSIBLE

   Due to the rain, it .... the children to play outside.

26   The idea that she can't teach Maths is completely wrong.

   TRUTH

   There .... the idea that she can't teach Maths.

27   'I didn't cheat in the exam!' said the student.

   DENIED

   The student .... in the exam.

Test 1

Visual materials for Paper 4: Speaking

Test 1

Part 2: Candidate A

> Why do you think these people have chosen to travel to work in this way?

Part 2: Candidate B

Why have the teachers organised their classes in this way?

Part 3

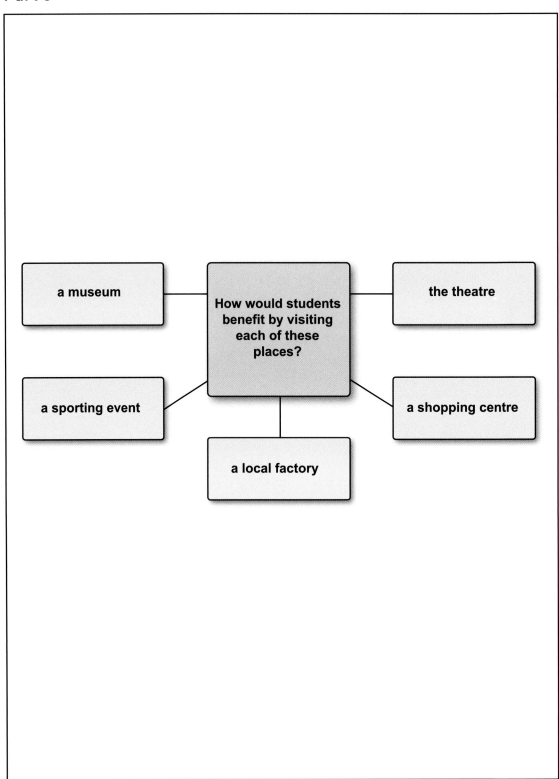

Test 2

Test 2

Part 2: Candidate A

What do you think these people are talking about?

Part 2: Candidate B

Why do people choose to shop in these places?

Part 3

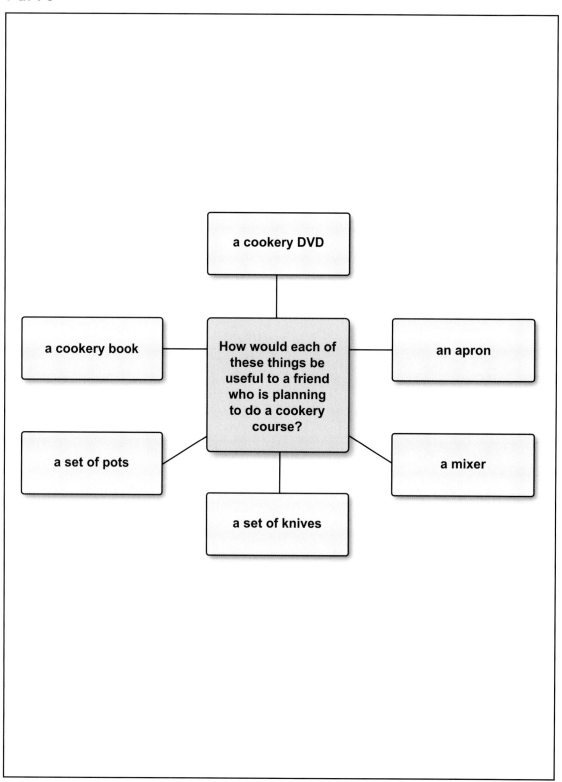

a cookery DVD

a cookery book

an apron

a set of pots

a mixer

a set of knives

How would each of these things be useful to a friend who is planning to do a cookery course?

Test 3

Test 3

Part 2: Candidate A

What do you think these people are waiting to do?

Part 2: Candidate B

Why do many people choose to do these jobs themselves?

Part 3

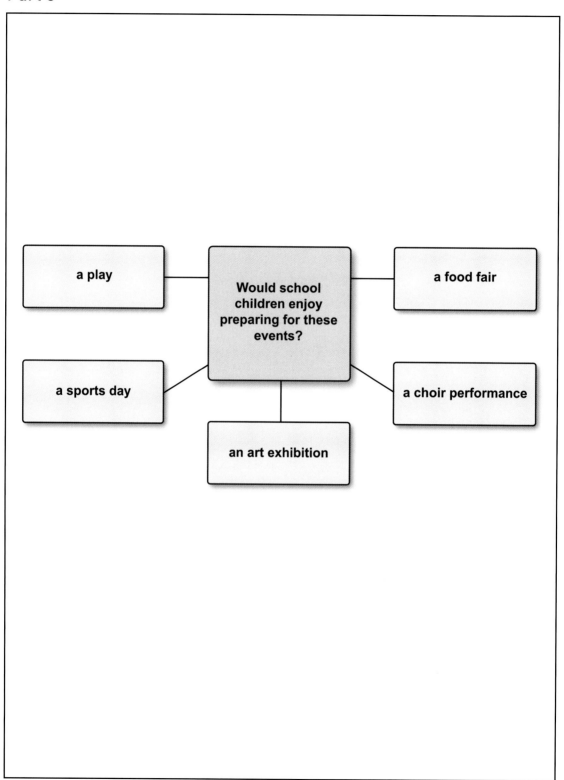

Test 4

Test 4

Part 2: Candidate A

Why do people choose to do activities like these?

Part 2: Candidate B

Which place would you prefer to live in?

Part 3

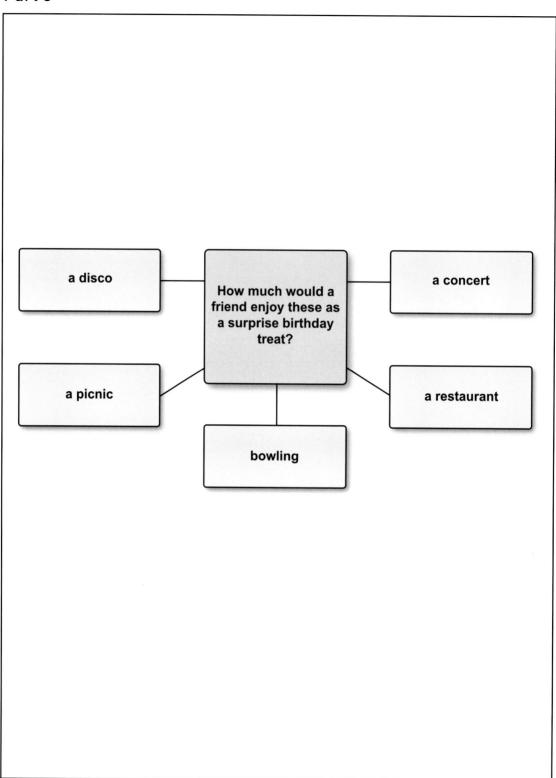

28 The teacher said I had to do my homework again.

INSISTED

The teacher .... doing my homework again.

29 They say the club is selling the player at the end of the season.

SAID

The club .... selling the player at the end of the season.

30 He constantly tells people how important his job is.

GOES

He always .... how important his job is.

Part 5

You are going to read an extract from a short story about a man who has lost his memory. For questions **31–36**, choose the best answer (**A**, **B**, **C** or **D**) according to the text.

Returning

It's nice to feel like a hero or to be the centre of attention every once in a while. Even better when you have a whole village waving you on, including the pretty girls. Walking barefoot down the worn dirt road, cheered on by the populace of Bradstone village, one would have thought that I should feel overwhelmed with pride and joy. Those feelings might have been nice, except for this one tiny fact: I had no idea why they were hailing me like I was their saviour. I had no clue where I was heading, even when I heard my name being shouted out upon entering the village.

Earlier, after slowly and painfully regaining consciousness in a grassy hollow beside the narrow road, the only important things I could remember were my name, Jonathan Grey, the pale face of a dark-haired child, and a horribly uncomfortable feeling that I had forgotten something which could result in life or death. So I had followed the road. What else was there for me to do? Shortly I noticed that I had somehow also come to lose track of my shoes.

I had ended up in Bradstone, a small cluster of wooden huts with one large brick building thrown in. People scrubbed at clothes, whilst mothers yelled after children or quieted their infants. Men gathered outside the larger building, talking in hushed voices. However, once I made my way around a bend in the road and entered their line of sight, all but a few left what they were doing and hurried over, throwing their hands in the air and screaming my name.

One older woman in particular came flying out from the hustle, flinging her small arms around my waist. 'You made it! I knew you were special, I just knew it!' she wailed between sobs. 'My baby is finally home!' At a loss for words, with no idea what to do, the best I could offer the crying woman was to wrap my arms around her, too, and keep them there until she settled down. When she did, she pulled back to look at me properly. 'How are you? Really? Oh, Ginger and Benjamin will be so pleased to have you back! You will have to report to Mr Fredrick first, so you'd best be off there now.'

I was not quite sure how to answer the woman's – my mother's? – questions, so I decided I best be honest. 'I'm sorry, but I'm not sure who Mr Fredrick is, or what I must report to him. And Ginger and Benjamin ...? Quite frankly I'm not even certain of my whereabouts for the past year.' At my confusion, the otherwise silent crowd gave a collective gasp. Their shock was mirrored on the old woman's face as she covered her mouth with her hand.

My mother took a deep breath, then took my hand to lead me into the village. Once at her little wooden hut, she took me inside and at once set to work, silently arranging the blankets and sheets in one corner of the room. 'Dinner shouldn't be long. Your father will be home soon as well, so get settled in. I'll be outside if you need me.' Taking one last look around, my mother let out a sigh before heading back to the door she'd just led me through. For the time being, home this would have to be. Breathing deeply, I gathered my courage and mentally prepared myself for what was now my new life.

31   What do we learn about Jonathan in the first paragraph?

  A   He feels proud as he enters the village.

  B   The villagers know who he is.

  C   He enjoys the welcome he receives.

  D   He has never been the centre of attention before.

32   What does Jonathan realise as soon as he regains consciousness?

  A   He doesn't have any shoes.

  B   He is in pain.

  C   Somebody has possibly died.

  D   He has no idea who he is.

33   What happens when Jonathan comes around the bend in the road?

  A   The villagers are able to see him.

  B   Everyone stops what they are doing.

  C   A few people run over to see him.

  D   Mothers tell their children to be quiet.

34   Why does Jonathan put his arms around the woman?

  A   He doesn't know what to say.

  B   He doesn't like to see her so emotional.

  C   She won't let him go.

  D   He is glad to have found her.

35   What do we learn when Jonathan answers his mother?

  A   He remembers his two brothers.

  B   The villagers are shocked by his answers.

  C   He doesn't want to upset the woman.

  D   He starts to recognise his mother.

36   How does Jonathan feel at the end of the extract?

  A   He isn't sure if he has the courage to start a new life.

  B   He knows that he has returned home.

  C   He decides to temporarily accept the situation he is in.

  D   He is worried about meeting his father.

Part 6

You are going to read an article about a girl who raises money to help people in need. Six sentences have been removed from the article. Complete the gaps (**37–42**) in the article with the sentences **A–G**. There is one extra sentence that you do not need to use.

One Card at a Time

In the late afternoon, fifteen-year-old Saanya Hasan Ali can often be found in the comfortable family room of her home in Potomac, Maryland. But she isn't doing homework and she isn't in front of a computer screen. **37** 'I just love arts and crafts,' exclaims Saanya, whose talent for designing and making greeting cards is matched by her dedication to helping children and families in need. During the past six years, she has raised an astonishing $26,000 through the sale of her cards, all while juggling the schedule of an active ninth-grader.

Saanya's success began in 2005, when her family was moving from Houston to Washington DC. 'My mother received an e-mail from friends who had just founded the Pennies for Education and Health (PEH) organisation. They were raising money for children in Gujarat, India to be able to go to school,' explains Saanya, who was nine at the time. Her mother, Salma, offered to donate $75 in Saanya's name, a sum that would pay for one child's schooling for a year. **38** 'I was in third grade then and I couldn't even wrap my mind around the fact that kids couldn't go to school over there,' she says.

Saanya and her mum unpacked one of the moving boxes filled with Saanya's crafts supplies, and she made cards to sell at a family wedding that summer. To her surprise, she earned $600 – enough to send eight children to school for the year. 'I kept on making cards and the following summer I was able to help support the kids for another year,' explains Saanya, who by then had established her own non-profit organisation called Children Helping Children. By 2007, she had earned a total of $10,000 for PEH. **39**

Encouraged by success, Saanya began to support other organisations, including SOS Children's Villages and the Central Asia Institute, which builds schools in Afghanistan and Pakistan, as well as earthquake relief efforts in Haiti, Pakistan and Japan. In 2007 she led a card-making workshop at the World Children's Festival in the National Mall in Washington DC, and in 2009 an article about her appeared in *Family Circle* magazine. **40** 'We had boxes full of supplies arriving at our home,' recalls Salma.

As demand for Saanya's cards rose, card making became a family-and-friends activity, too. 'I didn't want card making to become a chore because it is something I love to do and it makes me feel really good inside,' explains Saanya. **41** Her mother often helps assemble the cards now, and when her younger brother, Zayd, was seven, he used his toy dump truck to help clean up.

'I would love to continue making cards,' says Saanya. 'Now that I am in high school, I would also like to start giving talks in inner-city schools to try to inspire other kids to do their own projects. No matter who you are, there is always an opportunity to make a difference. **42** 'If everyone does their small part, it can grow into something beyond your expectations.'

A 'I couldn't do it without my family,' she emphasises, adding that it is often hard to find the time to make cards amid school and sports activities.

B One of her goals now, she says, is to support the schooling of these first eight children until they graduate from college.

C However, she didn't reach her target and decided to try a different approach.

D 'Making cards is my small effort,' she adds.

E She is cutting, drawing, measuring, gluing and folding, surrounded by a colourful chaos of paper, rubber stamps, buttons, stickers, ribbons and glitter.

F That not only brought new orders, but also unsolicited donations of card-making supplies.

G But Saanya decided she wanted to raise the money herself.

Part 7

You are going to read an article about four people who have taken up a hobby or interest. For each of the questions **43–52**, choose one of the people (**A–D**). You can choose the people more than once.

Which person has a colleague or colleagues who

is/are very poor at time-keeping?	43
is/are suffering from stress?	44
won an award?	45
is/are off sick at the moment?	46
is/are expecting a baby?	47
is/are working extra hours?	48
socialises/socialise with the writer away from work?	49
has/have recently transferred from another department?	50
isn't/aren't good at their job?	51
makes/make people laugh?	52

Colleagues

We asked readers to tell us about some of their favourite work colleagues – and others they'd rather not have. Here are some of their responses.

A I work with a fantastic group of colleagues. We've all been working for the company since it started and we're a close-knit unit. Business is going well at the moment and we're all rather busy, especially as one of us has been in hospital for a week. However, we work well as a team and we've been doing overtime since she's been off in order to get a project completed. We're getting paid for it but we would have been happy to put in the time for nothing in order to get the company out of a difficult situation. The company have invested in a leisure room where we can relax and play table tennis. We use it for informal meetings or somewhere to go to wind down. This is definitely not the kind of workplace where employees are likely to suffer from stress.

B To say I have a difficult working relationship with some of my colleagues is an understatement. I work in an office with six other people and four of us work together extremely well. One of my colleagues had a baby recently and we had to undertake her duties while the company advertised for a temporary replacement. Then we took on two new members of staff who have failed to fit into the team. Neither of them is prepared to do anything that isn't in their job description. To make matters worse, one of them arrives late most mornings and often leaves early, making a joke about how we should all do the same. But it's no laughing matter and only irritates us further. The other one has been called in to see the manager twice already regarding the poor quality of her work. All in all, it's been a bit of a disaster.

C I don't have problems with any of my colleagues; quite the opposite, in fact. I think we work very well together. I'm a mechanic and the team consists of myself, three other mechanics and the front of office staff, the people who deal with the customers. It's a small garage so we all know each other very well. One of the other mechanics is a friend of mine and we often see each other when we're not working. He's brilliant at his job and I've learnt a lot from him. Apparently, he won a regional competition when he was an apprentice. Mandy in reception is the person who does the most to guarantee there's always a great atmosphere at work. She's pregnant so we're going to have to do without her for a few months but we'll all be looking forward to her return later in the year.

D I've been a teacher for several years and I'm currently working in a college in Manchester, in the Maths department. I share a desk with Matthew, a nice man, but not someone who would win any awards for tidiness; his desk is always in a state. I haven't said anything to him about it as he seems rather anxious lately, what with family problems and lots of teaching hours. Then there's Kelly. She used to teach English but we were short of Maths staff so they moved her to our department as she's also qualified in this subject. Vince sits opposite me. He loves to get you in conversation even when you're busy preparing your next lesson, which only serves to make Matthew even more on edge. But Vince lightens the atmosphere with his jokes so we wouldn't want to be without him.

PAPER 2   WRITING

(1 hour 20 minutes)

Part 1

You **must** answer this question. Write your answer in an appropriate style (**140–190** words).

---

1   In your English class you have been talking about advertising.

Now your English teacher has asked you to write an essay.

Write an essay using **all** the notes and give reasons for your point of view.

Essay question

'There should be a ban on advertising to young children on TV.'
Do you think this is correct?

Notes

Write about:

1. *the pressure on parents to buy their children things*
2. *how children learn to deal with advertising*
3. *your own idea*

Now write your **essay**.

Part 2

You must write an answer to **one** of the questions **2–4**. Write your answer in an appropriate style (**140–190** words).

---

2   Your English teacher has asked you to write an article about the importance of having a hobby or interest. How do people benefit? Are certain hobbies or interests suitable for different ages?

       Write your **article**.

3   You see an advertisement in a newspaper for a waiter or waitress in a local restaurant. Read this part of the advertisement and then write a letter applying for the job.

> Are you the right person to join us in our new restaurant?
>
> If you are interested in applying to be a waiter or waitress, let us know why you think you would be a great addition to our team. Tell us about your work experience, your interests and anything else that will support your application.

       Write your **letter**.

4   You see this announcement in an international student magazine:

> **Do you visit a website on a regular basis?**
> **Is it a site our readers would find interesting?**
>
> You are invited to send in a review of a website you use regularly.
> The best submissions will be included in next month's magazine.

       Write your **review**.

PAPER 3   LISTENING

(approx. 40 minutes,
plus 5 minutes to transfer answers)

<h2 style="text-align:center">Part 1</h2>

14

You are going to hear people talking in eight situations. For questions **1–8**, choose the correct answer (**A**, **B** or **C**).

---

1   You hear a news report on the radio.

What has happened?

A   A car has been in a collision with a bus.

B   The trains are not running to the station.

C   A bridge has been hit by a train.

2   You hear a man talking to the receptionist in a leisure centre.

What does he have to do?

A   pay his membership fee

B   have his photograph taken

C   ask for his membership card to be posted

3   You hear a man and a woman talking about a friend.

What has the friend done?

A   He has broken his leg.

B   He has been on holiday.

C   He has started training.

4   You hear a conversation in a lift.

What does the woman say about her boss?

A   He expects her to work late.

B   He is kind and helpful.

C   He makes her feel guilty.

5 You hear a teacher talking to a student.

The student needs more time in order to

A finish writing her essay.

B get a book from the library.

C print her essay.

6 You hear an author talking on the radio about a book she has written.

What does she say about her research?

A It was more difficult than she had expected.

B She did some of it during a holiday.

C She interviewed Madeleine.

7 You hear a couple talking about their garden.

What does the woman say the man should do first?

A The hedge needs to be trimmed.

B The grass needs to be cut.

C The rubbish needs to be cleared away.

8 You hear a radio presenter talking about a new business.

What is on offer until 31 May?

A Job hunters can upload their CV.

B Registration on the website is free.

C Businesses can advertise at a cheaper rate.

Part 2

15

You are going to hear a teacher talking to students about how to read faster.
For questions **9–18**, complete the sentences. Use a word or short phrase.

Speed reading is about learning new [_____ **9**] , not just

reading in the same way but more quickly.

Start by [_____ **10**] your reading speed.

The most important thing is not to say the words [_____ **11**] .

To avoid pronouncing the words, run a [_____ **12**] along the

lines of text quite quickly.

Unlike verbs and nouns, many words in a text don't carry

[_____ **13**] .

Focus on groups of words, like blocks of [_____ **14**] seen from

an aeroplane.

Use paragraph [_____ **15**] to get an overall idea of the

general topic.

The [_____ **16**] sentences often give you an idea of the

meaning of a paragraph.

Re-reading parts of a text is a sign that you don't have the

[_____ **17**] to continue reading it.

Try to [_____ **18**] what you have read to see if you remember

the main points.

Part 3

16

You are going to hear five extracts in which people talk about a person they are close to. For questions **19–23**, choose from the list **A–H** the person each speaker describes. Use the letters once only. There are three letters that you do not need to use.

The speaker describes a person who

A   has been through a difficult situation.

B   always gives an honest opinion.

Speaker 1 | **19**

C   is good at making people feel happy.

Speaker 2 | **20**

D   is a good listener.

Speaker 3 | **21**

E   is confident.

Speaker 4 | **22**

F   has been generous with their time.

Speaker 5 | **23**

G   has a similar sense of humour to the speaker.

H   is forgiving when people make mistakes.

Part 4

17

You are going to hear part of an interview with a woman called Yvonne, who is a yoga instructor. For questions **24–30**, choose the correct answer (**A**, **B** or **C**).

24   What does Yvonne say about her first yoga sessions?

    A   Within two weeks her bad back was cured.

    B   She was surprised at how much she liked it.

    C   Her friend had to persuade her to go.

25   When did Yvonne become a yoga instructor?

    A   while she was teaching

    B   after she had left her teaching job

    C   after renting a room in a leisure centre

26   What does Yvonne like most about being an instructor?

    A   helping people overcome pain

    B   seeing people become enthusiastic about yoga

    C   teaching people something new

27   How has Yvonne's health benefitted from doing yoga?

    A   Her memory has improved.

    B   Her stress levels have fallen.

    C   Her blood pressure has improved.

28   What is Yvonne's advice?

    A   We should create a good work-life balance.

    B   We should choose friends who have a positive outlook on life.

    C   We should appreciate other people's good qualities.

29 What does Yvonne say about healthy eating?

    A We should take our time when eating.

    B Local produce usually costs more.

    C We should avoid foods like biscuits and chocolate.

30 According to Yvonne, where are you likely to get the best advice about yoga?

    A from a local school

    B from an instructor

    C from someone who has done yoga

PAPER 4   SPEAKING   (14 minutes)

Candidates take the test in pairs. There are two examiners. One of the examiners will talk to you. The other examiner will listen to you. You will get marks from both examiners.

Part 1

This part of the Speaking paper lasts for about two to three minutes.

One examiner will introduce himself/herself and the other examiner. He/She will then ask you and the other candidate what your names are. After that, he/she will ask you a few basic questions. These may be about yourself, your family, your home, your daily life, your interests, etc.

Part 2

This part of the Speaking paper lasts for about four minutes.

The examiner will give you two colour photographs and ask you to describe and compare them. You will have to speak for one minute. When you have finished, the examiner will ask the other candidate to comment on your photographs. He/She will have to speak for 30 seconds.

The examiner will then give the other candidate two different photographs on the same theme and ask him/her to describe and compare them. When the other candidate has finished, the examiner will ask you to comment on the photographs. You will have to speak for 30 seconds.

The photographs for Candidate A are on page xiv. The photographs for Candidate B are on page xv.

Part 3

This part of the Speaking paper lasts for about four minutes.

The examiner will give you and the other candidate instructions and some written prompts. He/She will then ask you to discuss a topic. You will have to exchange ideas with the other candidate, express and justify your opinions on the topic, agree and/or disagree, suggest, speculate and evaluate. Finally, you will have to negotiate with the other candidate to reach a decision about the topic. The prompts are on page xvi.

Part 4

This part of the Speaking paper lasts for about four minutes.

The examiner will ask you and the other candidate questions related to the topic of Part 3. You will have to express and justify your opinions, agree and/or disagree and speculate about the topic.

For examples of questions the examiner might ask you in the Speaking paper, please go to page 161.

For examples of answers that would get a good mark in the Speaking paper, please go to page 176.

Mini-dictionary

 Here are some of the more difficult words from the practice tests. Definitions and examples are from *Collins COBUILD Intermediate Learner's Dictionary*.

TEST 1

axle /ˈæksəl/ **(axles)** NOUN An **axle** is a rod connecting two wheels or two halves of a yo-yo. • *The position of the axle can be altered so that the wheel revolves at any angle.*

bar /bɑː/ **(bars, barring, barred)** VERB If you **bar** someone from doing something, you prevent them from doing it. • *My wife was barred from boarding the plane because the airline said her ticket hadn't been paid for.*

bear a grudge /ˌbeər ə ˈɡrʌdʒ/ **(bear grudges)** PHRASE If you **bear a grudge against** someone, you have unfriendly feelings towards them because they have harmed you in the past. • *It was an unfortunate misunderstanding but I bear you no grudge.*

black beetle /ˌblæk ˈbiːtəl/ **(black beetles)** NOUN A **black beetle** is a large brown insect that is sometimes found in warm places or where food is kept. • *Huge black beetles stalked around the bathroom.*

configuration /kənˌfɪɡʊˈreɪʃən/ **(configurations)** NOUN A **configuration** is an arrangement of a group of things. [FORMAL] • *an ancient configuration of giant stones*

dimension /daɪˈmenʃən dɪm-/ **(dimensions)** NOUN A particular **dimension** of something is a particular aspect of it. • *Many works of art have a spiritual dimension.*

domain /dəˈmeɪn/ **(domains)** NOUN Someone's **domain** is the area where they have control or influence. [FORMAL] • *Her office was her private, personal domain.*

embed /ɪmˈbed/ **(embeds, embedding, embedded)** VERB If you **embed** something, you fix it firmly and deeply into something. • *The European Central Bank is planning to embed microchips in Euro notes.*

emerge /ɪˈmɜːdʒ/ **(emerges, emerging, emerged)** VERB When something **emerges**, it comes into existence. [JOURNALISM] • *That idea first emerged in the early nineteenth century.*

expanse /ɪkˈspæns/ **(expanses)** NOUN An **expanse** of sea, sky or land is a very large area of it. • *He was staring out of the window at the grey expanse of the sea.*

fold /fəʊld/ **(folds, folding, folded)** VERB If a business, organisation, etc. **folds**, it is unsuccessful and has to close. • *About 330 companies have folded in the first six months of this year.*

frayed /freɪd/ ADJECTIVE If something such as cloth or rope is **frayed**, the threads at the edge have become worn and loose. • *He had frayed shirt cuffs.*

hectic /ˈhektɪk/ ADJECTIVE A **hectic** situation involves a lot of rushed activity. • *his hectic work schedule*

hobble /ˈhɒbəl/ **(hobbles, hobbling, hobbled)** VERB If you **hobble**, you walk with difficulty because you are in pain. • *She got up slowly and hobbled over to the coffee table.*

litter with /ˈlɪtə wɪð/ **(littered with)** PHRASAL VERB If a place is **littered with** things, there are a lot of them on it or in it. • *The table was littered with papers.*

nestle /ˈnesəl/ **(nestles, nestling, nestled)** VERB If you **nestle** something somewhere, you put it into a safe or sheltered place. • *She nestled the eggs in the straw in the basket.*

nibble /ˈnɪbəl/ **(nibbles, nibbling, nibbled)** VERB When animals **nibble** something, they take small bites of it quickly and repeatedly. • *The rabbit was nibbling a lettuce leaf.*

odour /ˈəʊdə/ (**odours**) NOUN An **odour** is a smell, especially one that is unpleasant.
• *The sharp odour of vomit hung in the air.*

recruit /rɪˈkruːt/ (**recruits**) NOUN A **recruit** is a person who has recently joined an organisation or army. • *They are training the new recruits.*

resurgence /rɪˈsɜːdʒəns/ NOUN If there is a **resurgence** in an attitude or activity, it reappears and grows. [FORMAL] • *Cinemas are currently enjoying a resurgence in popularity.*

sceptical /ˈskeptɪkəl/ ADJECTIVE If you are **sceptical** about something, you have doubts about it. • *He took a sceptical view of the Government's intentions.*

smudgy /ˈsmʌdʒi/ (**smudgier, smudgiest**) ADJECTIVE If something is **smudgy**, it is covered in dirty marks, especially where people have touched it. • *I went through the smudgy glass door without looking back.*

snatch /snætʃ/ (**snatches, snatching, snatched**) VERB If you **snatch** something, you take it or pull it away quickly. • *Mick snatched the cards from Archie's hand.*

survey /səˈveɪ/ (**surveys, surveying, surveyed**) VERB If you **survey** something, you look at or consider the whole of it carefully. • *He pushed himself to his feet and surveyed the room.*

vaudeville /ˈvɔːdəvɪl/ NOUN **Vaudeville** is a type of entertainment consisting of short acts such as comedy, singing and dancing. Vaudeville was especially popular in the early part of the twentieth century. [MAINLY US]
• *In 1901, she gave up vaudeville and set her sights on Broadway.*

TEST 2

abandon /əˈbændən/ NOUN If you do something **with abandon**, you do it in a carefree way. • *He danced with abandon.*

address /əˈdres/ (**addresses, addressing, addressed**) VERB If you **address** a problem, you try to understand it or deal with it. • *Mr King tried to address those fears when he spoke at the meeting.*

broker /ˈbrəʊkə/ (**brokers**) NOUN A **broker** is a person whose job is to buy and sell shares, foreign money or goods for other people.
• *She's a Wall Street broker.*

cite /saɪt/ (**cites, citing, cited**) VERB If you **cite** something, you quote it or mention it, especially as an example or proof of what you are saying. [FORMAL] • *She cited a favourite poem by George Herbert.* • *In my reply, I cited the time and details of the incident.*

discipline /ˈdɪsɪplɪn/ (**disciplines**) NOUN A **discipline** is an area of study, especially a subject of study in a college or university. [FORMAL] • *people from a wide range of disciplines*

discipline-hopping /ˈdɪsɪplɪnˌhɒpɪŋ/ NOUN **Discipline-hopping** is the practice of changing from one area of study to another, especially a subject of study in a college or university.
• *We want to promote discipline-hopping and knowledge transfer.*

ditch /dɪtʃ/ (**ditches**) NOUN A **ditch** is a long narrow channel cut into the ground at the side of a road or field. • *The car skidded off the road into a ditch.*

era /ˈɪərə/ (**eras**) NOUN An **era** is a period of time that is considered as a single unit because it has a particular feature.
• *He was arguably the finest British pianist of the post-war era.*

genome /ˈdʒiːnəʊm/ (**genomes**) NOUN In biology and genetics, a **genome** is the particular number and combination of chromosomes that are necessary to form the single nucleus of a living cell. [TECHNICAL]
• *Similarities between the human and rat genomes are as important as the differences.*

gravitate /ˈɡrævɪteɪt/ (**gravitates, gravitating, gravitated**) VERB If you **gravitate towards** a particular thing or activity, you are attracted by it and go to it or get involved in it. • *Traditionally young Asians in Britain have gravitated towards medicine, law and engineering.*

intellectual /ˌɪntɪˈlektʃʊəl/ ADJECTIVE **Intellectual** means involving a person's ability to think and to understand ideas and information. • *intellectual activities*

lens /lenz/ (**lenses**) NOUN If you examine or consider a subject through the **lens** of something, you examine or consider it in that way. • *Some people tend to look at the future through the lens of the past.*

limb /lɪm/ (**limbs**) NOUN Your **limbs** are your arms and legs. • *Get a free massage to ease your tired limbs.*

meet /miːt/ (**meets, meeting, met**) VERB If something **meets** a need, requirement or condition, it is satisfactory or sufficiently large to fulfil it. • *Many countries do not meet the conditions for World Bank loans.*

relocate /ˌriːləʊˈkeɪt/ (**relocates, relocating, relocated**) VERB If people or businesses **relocate**, they move to a different place. • *She had changed jobs and relocated to York.*

remuneration /rɪˌmjuːnəˈreɪʃən/ (**remunerations**) NOUN Someone's **remuneration** is the amount of money that they are paid for the work that they do. [FORMAL] • *the increase in the remuneration of the company's directors*

row /raʊ/ (**rows**) NOUN A **row** is a serious disagreement between people, organisations or countries, often one involving a noisy argument. • *The incident provoked a diplomatic row between the two countries.* • *Maxine and I had a terrible row about how I spent my money.*

sound /saʊnd/ (**sounder, soundest**) ADJECTIVE You can describe someone's mind or body as **sound** when it is in good condition. • *You should get plenty of sleep and exercise if you want a sound mind as well as a sound body.*

springboard /ˈsprɪŋbɔːd/ (**springboards**) NOUN If something is a **springboard for** something else, it makes it possible for that thing to happen or start. • *I hope this can be a springboard for future successes.*

subsidise /ˈsʌbsɪdaɪz/ (**subsidises, subsidising, subsidised**) VERB If a government, employer, etc. **subsidises** something, they pay part of the cost of it. • *The government continues to subsidise the production of eggs and beef.*

surge /sɜːdʒ/ (**surges, surging, surged**) VERB If people **surge** in a particular direction, they move suddenly and powerfully in that direction, usually in a crowd. • *The crowd surged into the station.*

tack /tæk/ (**tacks**) NOUN If you change **tack** or try a different **tack**, you try a different method for dealing with a situation. • *This report takes a different tack from the last one.*

test the water /ˌtest ðə ˈwɔːtə/ PHRASE If you **test the water**, you try to find out what reaction an action or idea will get before you do it or tell it to people. • *You should be cautious when getting involved and test the water before committing yourself.*

upfront /ˌʌpˈfrʌnt/ ADJECTIVE An **upfront** payment is made in advance and openly so that the person being paid can see that the money is there. • *Most rental houses require an upfront payment or a large deposit.*

vow /vaʊ/ (**vows**) NOUN A **vow** is a promise. • *I made a silent vow to be more careful in the future.* • *I took my marriage vows and kept them.*

wary /ˈweəri/ ADJECTIVE If you are **wary of** something, you are cautious because you do not know much about it and you believe it may be dangerous or cause problems. • *They were wary about giving him a contract.*

wind /wɪnd/ NOUN **Wind** is the ability to breathe easily when you are doing physical activity. • *He could hardly move because he suddenly lost his wind.*

TEST 3

broad daylight /brɔːd ˈdeɪlaɪt/ NOUN If you say that a crime happens in **broad daylight**, you are expressing your surprise that it is done during the day when people can see it, rather than at night. • *A man was attacked on a train in broad daylight.*

cherish /ˈtʃerɪʃ/ (**cherishes, cherishing, cherished**) VERB If you **cherish** something such as a hope or a pleasant memory, you keep it in your mind for a long period of time. • *We will cherish the memory of our visit to Ohio.*

cutting /ˈkʌtɪŋ/ (cuttings) NOUN A **cutting** is a piece of stalk that you cut from a plant and use to grow a new plant. • *Take cuttings from it in July or August.*

detoxify /diːˈtɒksɪfaɪ/ (detoxifies, detoxifying, detoxified) VERB If you **detoxify**, you do something to remove poisonous or harmful substances from your body. • *Many people try to detoxify once a year.*

diversion /daɪˈvɜːʃən/ (diversions) NOUN A **diversion** is a special route arranged when the normal route cannot be used. • *When the traffic slowed down too much, he had to make a diversion.*

embellishment /ɪmˈbelɪʃmənt/ (embellishments) NOUN An **embellishment** is a detail or decoration added to something to make it seem more attractive or interesting. • *I added a few further embellishments to my original story.*

engage in /ɪnˈɡeɪdʒ ɪn/ (engages in, engaging in, engaged in) PHRASAL VERB If you **engage in** something, you do it. [FORMAL] • *She had never engaged in any criminal activities.*

frame /freɪm/ (frames) NOUN You can refer to someone's body as their **frame**, especially when you are describing its general shape. • *her skinny frame*

gluttony /ˈɡlʌtəni/ NOUN **Gluttony** is the act or habit of eating too much and being greedy. • *illnesses associated with gluttony and poor diet*

gratuity /ɡrəˈtjuːɪti/ (gratuities) NOUN A **gratuity** is a gift of money to someone who has done something for you. [FORMAL] • *The porter expects a gratuity.*

literally /ˈlɪtərəli/ ADVERB You can use **literally** to emphasise a word or expression which is being used in a creative way to exaggerate a situation. Some careful speakers of English think that this use is incorrect. • *The views are literally breathtaking.*

loop /luːp/ (loops, looping, looped) VERB If you **loop** something such as a strap or piece of rope around an object, you tie a length of it in a loop around the object. • *He looped the rope over the wood.*

pigeon-hole /ˈpɪdʒɪn həʊl/ (pigeon-holes, pigeon-holing, pigeon-holed) VERB To **pigeon-hole** someone into doing something means to make them do it by restricting their choices. • *Chefs need to use exciting new ingredients and not be pigeon-holed into traditional methods and dishes.*

prospects /ˈprɒspekts/ PLURAL NOUN Someone's **prospects** are their chances of being successful. • *I worked abroad to improve my career prospects.*

recuperation /rɪˈkuːpəreɪʃən/ NOUN **Recuperation** is the recovery of your health or strength after you have been ill or injured. • *Sleep is necessary for recuperation.*

reflect /rɪˈflekt/ (reflects, reflecting, reflected) VERB When you **reflect on** something, you think deeply about it. • *I reflected on the child's future.*

restrict /rɪˈstrɪkt/ (restricts, restricting, restricted) VERB If you **restrict** something, you put a limit on it. • *Laws were passed to restrict foreign imports.*

run-through /ˈrʌn θruː/ (run-throughs) NOUN A **run-through** for a show, event, speech, etc. is a practice for it. • *Charles and Eddie are getting ready for their final run-through before the evening's recording.*

set up shop /ˌset ʌp ˈʃɒp/ PHRASE If you **set up shop** somewhere, you arrive there and unpack all your things. • *On previous camping trips we have set up shop in some pretty unwise places.*

sloth /sləʊθ/ NOUN **Sloth** is laziness, especially with regard to work. [FORMAL] • *He admitted a lack of motivation and a feeling of sloth.*

socket /ˈsɒkɪt/ (sockets) NOUN A **socket** is a hollow space in the human body where a moving part, such as an eye or an arm, fits. • *Her eyes were sunk deep into their sockets.*

spell /spel/ (spells) NOUN A **spell** is a period of time, especially a short one. • *After his spell in prison, Jake was thinner.*

stumbling block /ˈstʌmblɪŋ blɒk/ (stumbling blocks) NOUN A **stumbling block** is a problem which stops you from achieving something. • *Money remains the main stumbling block to an agreement.*

whip /wɪp/ (whips, whipping, whipped) VERB If the wind **whips** something somewhere, it makes it move there very quickly and suddenly. • *A fierce wind whipped the hair into his eyes.*

wind up /ˈwaɪnd ʌp/ (winds up, winding up, wound up) PHRASAL VERB If you **wind up** in a particular state, situation or place, you are in it after a series of actions or events, even though you did not intend to be. • *We just wound up feeling rather foolish.*

wrench /rentʃ/ (wrenches, wrenching, wrenched) VERB If you **wrench** something, you pull it suddenly and violently out of the place where it is. • *Croaker's arm was almost wrenched out of its socket.*

TEST 4

amid /əˈmɪd/ PREPOSITION If something happens **amid** other things, it happens while the other things are happening. [LITERARY] • *Those dreams seem to have been forgotten amid the difficulties of trying to deal with a change in lifestyle.*

assemble /əˈsembəl/ (assembles, assembling, assembled) VERB To **assemble** something means to fit the different parts of it together. • *Workers were assembling planes.*

at a loss /æt ə ˈlɒs/ PHRASE If you **are at a loss**, you do not know what to do or say in a particular situation. • *Amber stopped suddenly, at a loss for words.*

close-knit /ˈkləʊs ˌnɪt/ ADJECTIVE A **close-knit** group of people are closely linked, do things together and take an interest in each other. • *We're a very close-knit family.* • *Events over the last year have created a close-knit community.*

cluster /ˈklʌstə/ (clusters) NOUN A **cluster** is a small group of things. • *The shrub has clusters of tiny flowers in summer.*

emission /ɪˈmɪʃən/ (emissions) NOUN An **emission of** light, heat, radiation or a harmful gas is the release of it into the atmosphere. [FORMAL] • *The UK will find it very difficult to achieve its targets for reducing greenhouse gas emissions.*

found /faʊnd/ (founds, founding, founded) VERB When an organisation, company or city **is founded** by someone, they start it or create it. • *He founded the Centre for Journalism Studies at the university.*

gasp /gɑːsp, gæsp/ (gasps) NOUN If you give a **gasp**, you take a short, quick breath through your mouth, especially when you are surprised or in pain. • *A gasp of horror was heard.*

hail /heɪl/ (hails, hailing, hailed) VERB If a person or event **is hailed as** important or successful, they are praised publicly. • *US magazines hailed her as the greatest rock'n'roll singer in the world.*

hollow /ˈhɒləʊ/ (hollows) NOUN A **hollow** is an area that is lower than the surrounding surface. • *The water flows into a hollow and forms a pond.*

hustle /ˈhʌsəl/ NOUN **Hustle** is busy, noisy activity. • *She waited until they were beyond the hustle of the Saturday night traffic.*

infant /ˈɪnfənt/ (infants) NOUN An **infant** is a very young child or baby. [FORMAL] • *the relationship between mother and infant*

intimate /ˈɪntɪmət/ ADJECTIVE An **intimate** friendship or relationship is a good and close one. • *He formed an intimate friendship with Alfred Douglas.*

lose track of something /luːz ˈtræk əv/ PHRASE If you **lose track of** someone or something, you no longer know where they are. • *I lost track of one of the children I was looking after in the park.*

mirror /ˈmɪrə/ (mirrors, mirroring, mirrored) VERB If something **mirrors** something or someone else, it matches or expresses their qualities, features or feelings. • *The book mirrors my own interests and experiences.*

mortality /mɔːˈtælɪti/ NOUN The **mortality** in a particular place or situation is the number of people who die. • *the infant mortality rate in Britain*

pebble /ˈpebəl/ (pebbles) NOUN A **pebble** is a small stone. • *He kicked a pebble and heard it plop into the water.*

populace /ˈpɒpjʊləs/ NOUN The **populace** of a place is its people. [FORMAL] • *a large section of Pakistan's populace*

scrub /skrʌb/ (scrubs, scrubbing, scrubbed) VERB If you **scrub** something or if you **scrub at** it, you rub it hard in order to clean it, using a stiff brush and water. • *A woman in a white dress was on her knees, scrubbing at the floor.*

sob /sɒb/ (sobs) NOUN A **sob** is one of the noises that you make when you are crying. • *'I want to go home,' she said between sobs.*

specimen /ˈspesɪmɪn/ (specimens) NOUN A **specimen of** something is an example or small amount of it which gives an idea of the whole. • *Applicants have to provide a specimen of handwriting.*

understatement /ˈʌndəsteɪtmənt/ (understatements) NOUN An **understatement** is a statement which does not fully express the extent to which something is true. • *To say I'm disappointed is an understatement.*

unsolicited /ˌʌnsəˈlɪsɪtɪd/ ADJECTIVE Something that is **unsolicited** is given without being asked for and may not have been wanted. • *unsolicited advice*

wail /weɪl/ (wails, wailing, wailed) VERB If you **wail**, you cry loudly. • *The baby began to wail again.*

Audio script

 **Track 02**

TEST 1   PAPER 3 LISTENING

This is Cambridge English: First: Test 1, Listening.
I will now give you the instructions for this test.
I will introduce each part of the test and there will be time for you to look at the questions.
At the beginning of each piece you will hear this sound: ***

You are going to hear each piece twice. While you are listening, write your answers on the question paper. There will be five minutes at the end of the test for you to copy your answers onto the separate answer sheet.
There will now be a pause. If you have any questions, please ask them now because you will not be allowed to speak during the test.

Part 1

You are going to hear people talking in eight situations. For questions 1–8, choose the best answer, A, B or C.

1   *You hear a message on an answering machine.*

Man: Hi Chris ... Mark here ... I'm having a get-together at my house with a few friends this Saturday to celebrate my new job. It would be great to see you ... We're starting at about eight but feel free to arrive when you want. Why don't you stay the night so we can spend some time together the next day? Give me a ring and let me know if you can make it.

2   *You hear a conversation between a father and daughter.*

Father: So when are we going to get your computer looked at?
Daughter: Can we go to the shop on Friday? I'd sort it out myself but it's too heavy for me to carry.
Father: Are you coming home first or shall I meet you in town? I can bring the computer with me and see you in the shop.
Daughter: Um, I'll meet you there. I'll make an appointment and let you know what time to be there.

3   *You hear a lecturer making an announcement to students.*

Lecturer: I've just come to let you know about the arrangements for the exams next week. As you know, we've got building work going on at the moment and we don't want the noise to affect your concentration. There's a rumour going around that the exams are going to be cancelled but all we're doing is moving the exam room to the conference centre. If you don't know the building, ...

4 *You hear a radio interview with a man talking about tennis.*

Man: So anyway, the idea is we organise fun tennis matches for people who just want to turn up before or after work. We have all these tennis courts that are unused and it's a great way to get people active. We supply the rackets and balls – and some cold drinks. All people have to do is turn up and play for ... ten minutes, half an hour – however long they want.

5 *You hear a guide talking about an exhibition in an art gallery.*

Guide: ... And this is our latest installation by a new artist, Jason Roberts. We often host small installations but this is the first time we've had the pleasure of organising a show on such a large scale. The work takes up most of the main exhibition hall and visitors are invited to walk around and *through* the work, exploring the different effects the artist has produced depending on where the viewer is standing.

6 *You hear two people talking about a restaurant.*

Man: Have you tried that new restaurant? We went there last night. I'd heard it was good.
Woman: Yes, *we* went there last week. I had a lovely fish dish.
Man: I chose the fish too and yeah, it *was* delicious. But my wife complained that the portions were too small.
Woman: Well, it's not the kind of place that puts a lot of food on your plate. They just have a reputation for good quality food.

7 *You hear an interview with an author about his new book.*

Presenter: Your new book is unlike your previous works, isn't it?
Author: Yes, I'm known for crime thrillers and I've no intention of moving away from this genre but I couldn't get the idea of this historical romance out of my mind.
Presenter: Did you enjoy the change?
Author: It was different and the research into the historical facts was fascinating. I have to research a lot for crime stories but the historical angle was really enjoyable.

8 *You hear two students discussing a presentation.*

Boy: Well, I'm glad that's over. I've been worried about that presentation all week.
Girl: I was the same when I did mine. The night before I kept thinking: what could go wrong?
Boy: It's natural to feel anxious, isn't it? But the thought of standing up in front of people is worse than actually doing it. Towards the end, I was enjoying myself.
Girl: Well, the more times we do it, the easier it'll become.

This is the end of Part 1.

Part 2

You are going to hear a man talking about an activity he organises called orienteering. For questions 9–18, complete the sentences. Use a word or short phrase.
You have 45 seconds to look at Part 2.

Man: For those of you who haven't a clue what orienteering's about, this is a quick introduction. Orienteering is an adventure activity that involves getting from point A to point B. Organisers set up a course which can be anywhere out of doors: forests, open countryside, even in small, controlled environments such as a school playground. The courses have several stages between the start and end points, and the idea is to navigate around the course as quickly as possible, checking in at each stage in the correct order.

Distances vary but are often between one and ten kilometres. The level of difficulty is easy to identify as courses are colour coded. The brown and black courses are aimed at serious cross-country runners and are extremely challenging. However, for people new to orienteering, there are easier white and yellow courses. These courses are also popular with older people or people doing the course with young children, so if you simply want to take some gentle exercise, turn up and choose a suitable event.

On the day of the course, start times are staggered. In other words, people start at different times to make sure they find their way around the course by themselves. If times weren't staggered, people could just follow each other.

There's a small fee to register for an event. You will usually be given a free map when you register so you can follow the course. You'll need to bring a compass and it's a good idea to have a whistle. In some locations you won't be able to pick up a good mobile phone signal, so the whistle might be the only way of letting others know you're lost. You can also hire an emit card. This is an electronic gadget that allows you to record your time at each of the stages of the course.

Now, clothing. You'll need to come prepared for conditions that can vary depending on the course and the weather, and of course, you'll need strong walking boots or running shoes. It's also a good idea to wear long trousers as some courses can be through high grasses and sharp brambles which can scratch your legs otherwise.

And that's about it. If you check our website, you'll be able to see all the events taking place in your area, and get more information about orienteering generally. We're running an 'Introduction to Orienteering' event this Saturday and we organise weekly events at four different locations throughout the year. The next one takes place this coming Wednesday. Now, if anyone has any questions, I'll be happy to answer them.

You will now hear Part 2 again.

This is the end of Part 2.

 **Track 04**

Part 3

You are going to hear five extracts in which people talk about their reasons for doing voluntary work. For questions 19–23, choose from the list A–H the reason each speaker gives. Use the letters once only. There are three letters that you do not need to use.
You have 30 seconds to look at Part 3.

Speaker 1
Woman: I started doing voluntary work when I was seventeen. I wanted to gain some real-world skills, but I really like doing voluntary work and I'll carry on with it even after I get a full-time job. I've done some driving for the charity and I serve customers in the charity shop. I also do some marketing work for them online. The skills I've learnt will be useful when I look for a job after university.

Speaker 2
Man: To be honest, doing voluntary work's got nothing to do with me wanting to give something back to society. I just found myself feeling lost when I retired. I missed meeting friends at work and feeling part of a group. I've always been outgoing, so I decided to help out at my local community centre. Some days I serve tea and cakes in the centre's café or I do some gardening.

Speaker 3
Man: I've been unemployed for a while and I didn't want my children to see me sitting around when they got home from school. That's not the kind of example I want to give them. So I decided to do some voluntary work. It forces me to get up every morning and I get back after the children finish school so they can see I've done a day's work.

Speaker 4
Woman: I meet up with others to plant flowers in the centre of our town. Last year we entered for a 'Towns in Bloom' competition and got a bronze medal! Before we started, there was graffiti everywhere and vandalism. But we wanted people to take pride in the area – and it seems to be working! Now there are beautiful plants in the streets. The whole place looks and feels *much* nicer.

Speaker 5
Man: I have a boring job and I can't wait to get home every evening and leave the job behind. But I'm mad about old cars and at weekends I do volunteer work at a classic car fair. The fairs are very popular and things get busy, so I help out with anything that needs doing. I absolutely love it. I can indulge my passion and meet up with others who share the same love.

You will now hear Part 3 again.

This is the end of Part 3.

 **Track 05**

Part 4

You are going to hear part of a radio interview with a man called Simon, who is a usability expert. For questions 24–30, choose the correct answer, A, B or C.
You have one minute to look at Part 4.

Presenter: This evening we're talking to usability expert, Simon Baldwin. Simon, what exactly *is* usability?

Simon: It's about how objects are designed, and if they're designed in a way that makes them as effective and simple to use as possible. It's about designing from the point of view of the *user* rather than creating something that just *looks* attractive.

Presenter: Could you give us an example of good design?

Simon: Yes, sure. The traditional potato peeler, the old-fashioned knife with a shortish blade at a ninety-degree angle and a slot down the length of the blade. You can see by looking at it how it works. People have been using it for years because it's uncomplicated – and it works. It looks unimaginative but unlike some modern gadgets, it's very easy to use.

Presenter: What about an example of a poor design?

Simon: Yes ... I was trying to withdraw money from a cash machine at my bank the other day. They'd changed the order of instructions on the screen so that the most common choices – like asking for money – were at the top of the list, which was great. But the screen had also been changed. It was at an angle that reflected light so badly that it was difficult to see.

Presenter: What kind of things do you assess for usability?

Simon: Well, I used to work with companies making household appliances. But recently usability has become important in software design and websites, which is the area I'm involved in now.

Presenter: What's the biggest mistake made by website designers?

Simon: There are some technical issues which are important but ... I suppose to put things simply, you *must* be able to find your way around a website easily. Anything that makes this difficult is going to cause problems. People shouldn't rush the planning stage.

Presenter: Is it a difficult area to find work in?

Simon: Quite the opposite, actually. In the past companies were less concerned about usability but now they realise that if their site doesn't offer users what they want easily, they'll go elsewhere. So good web design is now seen as important and there are lots of people helping companies to do this.

Presenter: So how do people get into the field of usability?

Simon: You need to be comfortable with computers if you're interested in web design, though you don't need to be a programmer. People get into usability from different backgrounds rather than entering it directly from university. You might have experience in marketing or customer service, or you might have a background in graphic design. These are all common ways into usability.

You will now hear Part 4 again.

This is the end of Part 4.
There will now be a pause of five minutes so that you can copy your answers onto the separate answer sheet. Make sure you follow the numbering of all the questions. I will let you know when there is one minute left.

 **Track 06**

TEST 2 PAPER 3 LISTENING

This is Cambridge English: First Certificate in English: Test 2, Listening.
I will now give you the instructions for this test.
I will introduce each part of the test and there will be time for you to look at the questions.
At the beginning of each piece you will hear this sound: ***

You are going to hear each piece twice. While you are listening, write your answers on the question paper. There will be five minutes at the end of the test for you to copy your answers onto the separate answer sheet.
There will now be a pause. If you have any questions, please ask them now because you will not be allowed to speak during the test.

Part 1

You are going to hear people talking in eight situations. For questions 1–8, choose the best answer, A, B or C.

1 *You hear a conversation between a man and a woman at a party.*

Woman:	Hi. We met recently at a conference in Manchester, didn't we?
Man:	Yes, that's right. I was there to give a talk on property development for the company I work for.
Woman:	That sounds exciting. Do you like the job?
Man:	Yes. The company is based in London so I have to commute from Birmingham every day but it doesn't take too long – and I enjoy what I do.

2 *You hear an interview on the radio with a cyclist.*

Presenter:	... And I understand you're about to start on another journey?
Cyclist:	Not for a few months yet. I'm still recovering from the last trip.
Presenter:	That was through Europe, wasn't it?
Cyclist:	Well, part of Europe. From the north of Spain. I started across the border in France, down through Spain to the south of the country. It was a fantastic trip and easier than my previous ride in Switzerland, when I had trouble ...

3 *You hear a guide talking to visitors in an art gallery.*

Guide:	Welcome to the Arcon Gallery. This afternoon we'll be looking at the new exhibition as well as our permanent collections. If you've been here before, you'll notice the place has been decorated, so it's easier to appreciate the paintings. Unfortunately, the builders also damaged the beautiful tiled flooring there ... And we won't be going into the main hall as the paintings there are being re-arranged. Anyway, if you'll follow me ...

4 *You hear a man talking to a police officer.*

Police officer: Is everything all right, sir?

Man: Not really. I'm locked out of my car. We parked it here and went into town but then my wife couldn't find the keys. She's gone to see if she's left them in one of the shops.

Police officer: Do you need the number of an emergency service?

Man: Thanks, but I should be OK. My wife will be back soon – and we have a spare set of keys at home.

5 *You hear a customer talking to a waiter in a café.*

Waiter: Good morning, madam. Are you ready to order?

Customer: Um, I'd like a cup of coffee, please, and something to eat. Have you got a menu?

Waiter: Here you are. We've got some lovely soup today.

Customer: Ooh, yes, it smells fantastic. Um … and the sandwiches look lovely too. Um … I think I'll have one of them … I'd better avoid the cream cakes, though they *do* look delicious …

6 *You hear a student leaving a message on an answering machine.*

Student: Hi Mum. The exams begin first thing tomorrow morning – and you know what I'm like at that time of the day. I hope I can concentrate. I've done loads of revision but I don't feel ready. I, er, I missed a couple of lectures this term and I don't know enough about one particular topic. Anyway, I'll, er, I'll call you tomorrow to let you know how it went.

7 *You hear a woman called Judy talking on the phone to her friend Martin.*

Judy: Hi Martin. It's Judy. How are you?

Martin: I'm fine, thanks. Are we still going to the party together?

Judy: I'm going, yes, but don't worry about giving me a lift. I'm going to share a taxi with my flatmate. But I was going to ask if I could pop round later to collect my phone. I left it there yesterday.

Martin: Yes, sure. I'll see you later.

8 *You hear a footballer talking about his career.*

Presenter: Well, Dave, how do you feel when you look back at your career?

Footballer: I've been fortunate enough to play for some top teams. It's a pity I was injured earlier in the season. If I hadn't missed those games, I might have broken the club record for most games played. I've had a few yellow cards, sure, but my discipline record has been good, I think. All in all, I'm most pleased about being voted player of the year last season.

This is the end of Part 1.

 **Track 07**

Part 2

You are going to hear a man talking about courses in Internet security. For questions 9–18, complete the sentences. Use a word or short phrase.
You have 45 seconds to look at Part 2.

Man: Hello everyone. It's great to have a chance to talk to you about Internet safety. There are many reasons for going online, as you've discovered on this course, but it's also important to be aware of the dangers.

Starting next week, we're running some sessions about online safety in the local library and we'll be looking at how to create strong passwords. Some users make it simple for anyone to guess a password: they use things like their child's name or simply the word 'password', so I'll be showing you how to make things difficult for the criminal.

Then the week after, we'll turn to something called phishing. This is where criminals try to trick you into giving up personal information by claiming to be a well-known bank, for example. One way they do this is by sending an email telling you your bank account details need updating. Or you might get a message saying you've bought something and they want you to confirm that it's correct. So I'll be telling you what to do and what *not* to do when you get a message like this.

Next month we'll be looking at how to keep your computer safe from viruses. If you've bought a computer recently, it may well have come with Internet security installed, but have you checked whether the software is up-to-date? And if you use wireless networks in your house or in a pubic space, this has its own security issues.

What's next … Oh yes. Um, you've already had some training in using Twitter and Facebook but it's important to practise common sense with social media. In another session we'll be looking at what information people choose to share about themselves, their friends and family. This can be sensitive information so it's important to be familiar with the privacy settings of various social media sites. Essentially, you'll be able to decide who can see the things you post on them, but you might want to consider whether that photo you love is appropriate for pubic viewing. This issue is particularly important for young people so if you have grandchildren, have a word with them after the session.

And last but not least, we'll explore how to make sure your photos and music don't go up in smoke if your computer crashes. A couple of years ago I had three computers die on me in a single week so you really do need to make sure your files are backed up. If you're interested in any of these sessions, I have leaflets here with dates and times …

You will now hear Part 2 again.

This is the end of Part 2.

 **Track 08**

Part 3

You are going to hear five extracts in which people talk about a journey they have made. For questions 19–23, choose from the list A–H the reason each speaker gives for enjoying the journey. Use the letters once only. There are three letters that you do not need to use.
You have 30 seconds to look at Part 3.

Speaker 1

Man: I travelled to Greece one year, before I went to university. I didn't have much money so I went by coach. We travelled non-stop from London to Athens so we slept on the coach. It was a relaxing way to travel and it didn't take any planning at all. I just bought the ticket and that was that. And best of all, I finished three books on the journey!

Speaker 2

Woman: My family and I went to France last year. We took the car and drove through towns and villages you wouldn't get to see if you used public transport. We wanted to check routes beforehand but our Internet connection was down. I ended up buying a couple of maps. I had to get used to driving on the right-hand side of the road but it was a lovely holiday.

Speaker 3

Woman: I always prefer to travel by train. It's such a great way to meet people. I've just returned from a train journey through Sri Lanka. Not very comfortable, but I loved getting into conversation with the local people and finding out more about them. Travelling by train is the best way to see a country. Going by plane means you miss all the interesting places on the way to your destination.

Speaker 4

Man: I went away with a friend a few years ago in his mobile home. We just took our time and stopped off at places that looked nice – and we didn't need to worry about booking into hotels. We got to see some *beautiful* countryside and the views were unbelievable. It was the first trip I'd ever made where I wasn't concerned about when we were going to arrive.

Speaker 5

Woman: My husband and I flew to America last year even though I hate flying. But the flight attendants were wonderful. They made it their job to keep me calm and put me at ease. I still don't like flying, though. All the passengers are squeezed into tiny spaces. You enjoy the journey more in a car or a train. You get a real sense that you're *travelling*. You just don't get the same feeling in a plane.

You will now hear Part 3 again.

This is the end of Part 3.

 **Track 09**

Part 4

You are going to hear part of a radio interview with a woman called Claire, who does mountain running. For questions 24–30, choose the correct answer, A, B or C.
You have one minute to look at Part 4.

Presenter: Today I'm talking to Claire Bradshaw about mountain running. Claire, it sounds exhausting, running up and down mountains.

Claire: Well, like any sport, it takes practice but everyone has to start somewhere. Actually, calling it 'mountain running' makes it sound worse than it is. Most people run up and down *hills* rather than mountains – or *several* hills in one session.

Presenter: Whew! Do a lot of people do mountain running?

Claire: Yes. The runs take place in countryside with the right landscape – areas like the Lake District and the Highlands of Scotland are very popular. But this doesn't stop people from the city talking part. For example, I drive to *my* club from my city apartment. And there are *hundreds* of clubs so you'll probably find one not too far from home.

Presenter: Where did it originate?

Claire: Well, there are records of people doing this going back nearly a thousand years. It's always been associated with country fairs and festivals. People would challenge each other to run to the top of a hill and back again. Over time it became formalised and nowadays a run is usually a stand-alone national event. Or sometimes an international event.

Presenter: Hmm. What are the tougher courses like?

Claire: There's a race called The Dragon's Back, which takes place over five days and over a distance of 200 miles across the Welsh mountains. But before listeners sign up for it, I should point out that only people with lots of experience are allowed to enter.

Presenter: How can you get started in the sport?

Claire: Well, you start with something easy and work your way up to more challenging runs, depending on your fitness and motivation. If you're keen to enter races, you'll find they're graded in terms of distance and height. But just as people start jogging without necessarily wanting to run a marathon, you don't *have* to enter mountain running races.

Presenter: How does mountain running differ from road running in terms of difficulty?

Claire: Um, in some ways, it's less of a strain on your body. A lot of running injuries are due to the repetitive nature of the movement, the repeated impact on the same part of the foot when running along hard roads, whereas in mountain running, you're constantly having to adjust your footing or body to deal with different surfaces.

Presenter: But surely it's very demanding?

Claire: Yes. Even experienced runners need to get used to running over rough grass, rocky paths, up hillsides or through mountain streams. And running downhill is more difficult than running uphill. You find yourself going faster and faster when running downhill, which can be frightening when you're not used to it.

You will now hear Part 4 again.

This is the end of Part 4.

There will now be a pause of five minutes so that you can copy your answers onto the separate answer sheet. Make sure you follow the numbering of all the questions. I will let you know when there is one minute left.

 **Track 10**

TEST 3   PAPER 3 LISTENING

This is Cambridge English: First Certificate in English: Test 3 Listening.
I will now give you the instructions for this test.
I will introduce each part of the test and there will be time for you to look at the questions.
At the beginning of each piece you will hear this sound: ***

You are going to hear each piece twice. While you are listening, write your answers on the question paper. There will be five minutes at the end of the test for you to copy your answers onto the separate answer sheet.
There will now be a pause. If you have any questions, please ask them now because you will not be allowed to speak during the test.

Part 1

You are going to hear people talking in eight situations. For questions 1–8, choose the best answer, A, B or C.

1 *You hear two people talking about a film they have just seen.*

Man: Well, I don't understand what the fuss was about. I thought it was disappointing.

Woman: Hmm, it wasn't as good as his earlier work but I enjoyed it. It was longer than his other films but I only noticed it when we came out and I checked my watch.

Man: The seats didn't help. I've never been so uncomfortable.

Woman: Mine was OK, but those people behind us were really annoying, chatting through the whole film.

2 *You hear a woman talking on the radio about a business she runs.*

Presenter: ... And your business is doing well?

Woman: Yes, very well, especially if you consider we only started the company a year ago. In fact, we're taking on two trainees over the next few months.

Presenter: Hmm. And you're about to launch a new product?

Woman: It's already available, actually. That's one of the reasons we're taking people on. My husband and I need to spend more time meeting with retailers and getting our products into their shops.

3 *You hear a message on an answering machine.*

Man: Hi Aaron. I'm calling to let you know we need to get to the station by two thirty. We had to rearrange the meeting as a few people couldn't make it. It now begins at five but I think we should be there by four thirty to make sure all the technology works. I'll meet you at the station and we can travel up together. See you then.

4 *You hear a man and a woman talking about the man's car.*

Woman: Have you sorted your car out?

Man: Yes, though it's costing me a fortune. We found out why it wouldn't start and got it fixed. The next problem was the insurance. My son uses it now and it cost about fifty per cent more to get it insured.

Woman: Hah! But you're back on the road, right?

Man: Not quite. My son's taken it on holiday so I'm using my bike to get around.

5 *You hear a message from a school secretary on an answering machine.*

Woman: Hello, it's Ambrose School here. I'm calling about the school trip tomorrow. The coach leaves at nine thirty and returns at three thirty so you can collect Sam then. We'll be using the leisure centre's catering facilities. They supply the children with a packed lunch so Sam won't need to bring any food with him. He'll need a sun hat, though, and sun cream, as it's going to be a hot day. Thanks.

6 *You hear a customer talking to a shop assistant.*

Assistant: Did you find the changing rooms, sir?

Customer: Yes, thanks. I tried this suit on but the trousers are too big. Have you got them in a smaller size?

Assistant: Not at the moment, but we're getting a new delivery in on Friday. Or we could get the trousers altered for you.

Customer: Hmm. I love the suit but I'm not in a hurry for it. I'll pop back on Friday.

7 *You hear a shopkeeper being interviewed on the radio.*

Presenter: ... And you've got the support of other shopkeepers?

Shopkeeper: Yes, and we're doing all we can to increase trade – special offers, late night opening ... But if we can't even get people into the high street, we've got no chance.

Presenter: But what's wrong with the bus? It's a good service, isn't it?

Shopkeeper: People want convenience and if they've got nowhere to park, they'll go elsewhere. We really need to provide a space for them.

8 *You hear an employee talking to her boss.*

Boss: Morning, Mary. Everything OK?

Mary: Not really. I told you about the problem I had getting a replacement computer from the technicians when mine stopped working. Well, they sorted that out but they still haven't given me my account for the Intranet. I can't work from home until they do.

Boss: OK, I'll talk to their manager.

Mary: Thanks. I just want to be able to get on with my job and transfer some files from home.

This is the end of Part 1.

 **Track 11**

Part 2

You are going to hear a college manager telling new members of staff about training opportunities. For questions 9–18, complete the sentences. Use a word or short phrase. You have 45 seconds to look at Part 2.

Manager: ... I hope you're all enjoying your new jobs here at the college. Now I'd like to tell you a little about our staff development training programmes. We're proud of our work in this area and we've appeared as a case study in several national reports.

We all operate in an ever-changing world and therefore our training programmes are vital. It means we can support you so that you have the skills and knowledge required to keep you up-to-date in your area of work. This means you can improve your career prospects, whether by getting promotion within the college or finding a job elsewhere. You will also function better as a team player and work more efficiently and effectively. Most importantly, our staff training programmes make sure our students get excellent service from us.

So how does professional development work here? To begin with, we expect you to attend team meetings. These take place in the last week of each term; so three times a year. They will give you the chance to share experiences with colleagues, identify problem areas and notify us of any training requirements. If training is required, the college will fund the costs in full. The members of staff who attend training sessions will be asked to complete a feedback form about their experiences and to share this with their colleagues at their next team meeting. The college also identifies areas where all members of staff can benefit from training. This could come about as a result of the introduction of new technology or new government regulations.

Which brings me to our all-college training days. These take place twice a year and are held over an entire day. No classes take place on these days. Members of staff can choose from a series of events the ones they'd like to attend. These days are meant to be fun as well as informative, and the café will provide a free meal from a special menu.

Finally, each team will be given the chance to enjoy an 'away day'. These are full day events, sometimes held at a hotel or leisure centre. However, some teams like to spend part of the day doing team-building activities such as ice-skating, rock climbing or orienteering. Others choose to spend the 'away day' at the home of one of the team. The college covers all the costs for these events, and if you use the home of a member of staff, you will be given £100 to cover catering costs.

Now, any questions?

You will now hear Part 2 again.

This is the end of Part 2.

 **Track 12**

Part 3

You are going to hear five extracts in which people talk about money.
For questions 19–23, choose from the list A–H the attitude each speaker has towards money.
Use the letters once only. There are three letters that you do not need to use.
You have 30 seconds to look at Part 3.

Speaker 1

Man: I don't think I'm motivated by money but I'd like to be able to splash out now and again or take the children out for a treat. Not too often though; I wouldn't want to spoil them. On the other hand, when money is short, it can cause problems. When I was unemployed, my wife and I argued more than usual ... not having enough to pay for holidays, that kind of thing.

Speaker 2

Woman: It must be great to be rich. Never having to get up for work on a Monday morning again. If I came into a lot of money, I'd see the world – do a one-year cruise. Some people say they wouldn't feel comfortable with all that money but it wouldn't bother me. I'd give some to my friends, donate some to charity. I'd enjoy being generous.

Speaker 3

Woman: When people think about having lots of money, it's often to do with material things. But I think it's about sorting out the things that make you feel safe. For example, you could take out private health care for you and your family and get the best treatment in case of illness. You could pick the best schools for your children. But whether those things make you *happier*, I don't know.

Speaker 4

Man: I've always been careful with money and over the years I've got most of the things I need without owing money to anyone. That's something I've always wanted to avoid at all costs. Having more money wouldn't make a great deal of difference to me. Some people would say being rich enables you to leave money to your children but I'd like to see my kids work for the things they need in life.

Speaker 5

Woman: I don't earn a great deal, so money has always been tight. I think I'd *enjoy* having more to spend. But if I came into a lot of money, I don't think it would make me a different person. I wouldn't waste it or spend it on things I don't need. In fact, unless I told them, I don't think my friends or relatives would know I'd become rich overnight.

You will now hear Part 3 again.

This is the end of Part 3.

 **Track 13**

Part 4

You are going to hear part of a radio interview with a woman called Molly, who flies commercial aeroplanes. For questions 24–30, choose the correct answer, A, B or C.
You have one minute to look at Part 4.

Presenter: In the latest of our interviews with women in male-dominated professions, I'm talking to Molly, a commercial airline pilot. Molly, did you always want to fly?

Molly: I did, yes. My father worked in air traffic control so planes were always a topic of conversation in our house. At first, I wanted to do his job but then there were a few holidays abroad. That's when I developed an interest in becoming a professional pilot.

Presenter: And did your parents encourage you? After all, it's a very male-dominated profession.

Molly: My parents were fantastic in that way. They were keen for me to explore various career options and we spent time investigating what the life of a pilot is like. Over ninety per cent of pilots are men, and that figure would have been even higher when I was a child. But my parents didn't see that as a reason for me not to follow my passion.

Presenter: So how did you get started?

Molly: It wasn't easy. I did well at school and went to university. Actually, a degree isn't necessary to become a pilot but I wanted a backup in case the flying ambition didn't work out. Then I spent a few years working in sales. It was boring but I needed to save enough money to go to training school to get my private pilot's licence. I then needed to do at least 150 hours of flying time.

Presenter: So was that all you needed to become an airline pilot?

Molly: No! That's when the hard work *starts*. I had to do a lot more training. There are theory tests, then training that includes flying a multi-engine plane. Then you move on to the full commercial licence itself. Taken altogether, this training takes about 75 hours and costs a lot of money.

Presenter: And then six months ago you started to fly professionally?

Molly: Yes. I applied to a major airline and they took me on. I'm now a first officer, which means I'm second in command. I get to fly the plane for certain sections of journeys; the captain and I decide who will fly which sections before we take off.

Presenter: Hmm. So where does your career go from here?

Molly: The next step is senior first officer. That will allow me to fly to more airports and under different weather conditions. Eventually, I can apply to become a captain.

Presenter: What would you say to people who want to become a pilot?

Molly: If you're not obsessed about becoming a pilot, forget it. Getting all your training and flying qualifications costs a lot of money so unless you have a well-paid job to pay for your lessons, you can end up in debt. But if you're determined, go for it.

You will now hear Part 4 again.

This is the end of Part 4.
There will now be a pause of five minutes so that you can copy your answers onto the separate answer sheet. Make sure you follow the numbering of all the questions. I will let you know when there is one minute left.

 Track 14

TEST 4 PAPER 3 LISTENING

This is Cambridge English: First Certificate in English: Test 4, Listening.
I will now give you the instructions for this test.
I will introduce each part of the test and there will be time for you to look at the questions.
At the beginning of each piece you will hear this sound: ***

You are going to hear each piece twice. While you are listening, write your answers on the question paper. There will be five minutes at the end of the test for you to copy your answers onto the separate answer sheet.
There will now be a pause. If you have any questions, please ask them now because you will not be allowed to speak during the test.

Part 1

You are going to hear people talking in eight situations. For questions 1–8, choose the best answer, A, B or C.

1 *You hear a news report on the radio.*

Reporter: And now some traffic news. Due to a bridge collapse there are no trains into Norcombe Central Station until further notice. Extra buses have been laid on but more people are using their cars to get into town so all main routes are now extremely busy. Police recommend that anyone who doesn't have a good reason to go into town should avoid the area for the time being.

2 *You hear a man talking to the receptionist in a leisure centre.*

Receptionist: Good morning, sir. How can I help you?

Man: Yes … My name's Paul Flynn. I recently renewed my membership and I was told I'd get my new card in the post. That was three weeks ago and it still hasn't arrived.

Receptionist: Ah yes ... Um, Mr Flynn ... I've got your membership card here. We need an up-to-date photo before we can release it.

Man: Hmm. I wasn't told that. I'll have to get one taken.

3   *You hear a man and a woman talking about a friend.*

Woman: Have you seen Jim since it happened?

Man: Yes. I've been round his house a couple of times. He was going to spend his holiday touring with his football team but he had to pull out.

Woman: When will he be able to play again?

Man: It'll be a couple of months before he can start training. Probably longer before he can play for the team. It takes months for a broken leg to recover fully.

4   *You hear a conversation in a lift.*

Man: So, how's the new department?

Woman: Not too bad. My colleagues are kind and helpful but I've had some issues with the boss.

Man: Really? He's supposed to be great to work for.

Woman: Well, maybe it's me, then, but he's always looking at his watch when you go home at the end of the day. I don't know how long he expects people to work for but he's not going to make *me* feel guilty.

5   *You hear a teacher talking to a student.*

Teacher: ... But I told you the deadline was twelve, Susan.

Susan: I know, and I did try to get the essay finished on time. And it's not as if I haven't finished. It's ready to go but I need to get a hard copy.

Teacher: How much time do you need?

Susan: I just need to wait for the library to open after lunch so I can get the file printed ...

6   *You hear an author talking on the radio about a book she has written.*

Presenter: ... It's certainly a well researched biography. Did the research take a lot of time?

Author: It did, and it entailed travelling to Glasgow, where Madeleine was born, and then to Madrid, where she spent her married life. Fortunately, I was able to build the trips to Spain around family holidays. My husband entertained the children while I interviewed people who knew Madeleine. I was expecting this to be difficult as I don't speak Spanish but it turned out OK.

7   *You hear a couple talking about their garden.*

Man: So, what needs doing?

Woman: Well, the grass needs cutting, the hedge needs trimming and there's a pile of rubbish at the end of the garden that needs throwing out.

Man: But I've only got an hour. I'm playing golf this afternoon.

Woman: Well, I can do the grass later, but I'm not tall enough to do the hedge ... Oh! We *do* need to get that rubbish cleared before Bob and Mary come round for dinner tonight.

8 *You hear a radio presenter talking about a new business.*

Presenter: ... And now some news for job hunters and businesses looking for new staff. St John's Recruitment Office opened last week in the centre of town. For one month only, until 31 May, local businesses can advertise vacancies for half price. *And* ... if you're looking for work, you can register on their website. Upload your CV and search for what's available in your area. The service is free for job hunters.

This is the end of Part 1.

 **Track 15**

Part 2

You are going to hear a teacher talking to students about how to read faster. For questions 9–18, complete the sentences. Use a word or short phrase.
You have 45 seconds to look at Part 2.

Teacher: ... OK. Now I did promise I was going to give you some tips about improving your reading speed. A lot of people get the wrong impression when they think about speed reading. They imagine it means doing what you normally do, just faster. But actually, you read more quickly by learning new techniques and reading in a different *way*.

First, you need to find out how fast you can read already by timing yourself. Read something with comprehension questions so you'll know if you've actually understood what you've read. Then after a few months of training, try a similar test and see if you're faster. There are lots of these tests online.

Now ... techniques. My number one tip is: don't say the words out loud as you read. It's much faster to read in your head so keep your lips closed. To help you not to voice words, take a pen and run the tip quickly along the line you're reading, paying attention to the words as you do so. The moving pen will force your eye to keep moving. Eventually, you'll find a speed that you feel comfortable with but which will also be too fast for you to 'speak' the words.

Another thing. In order to understand a text, we don't need to read *every* word. Words like 'a', 'the' and 'did' don't carry any meaning so focus on key words, like nouns and verbs. Eventually, you should try to avoid reading individual words and instead focus on groups of words. Imagine you're zooming out or away from the text, seeing it from further away, just like when we're in an aeroplane ... When we're low down we see individual buildings but as we get higher, we see *blocks* of houses. Do the same when you read.

Another tip is to use features of the text to help you get an understanding. Paragraph headings will give you an idea of the general topic; scan the text for these before you read in more detail. Also, within each paragraph, the opening sentences will often tell you all you need to know. Now and again, you might need to get further details; that's when you read the rest of the sentences.

Finally, get out of the habit of *re*-reading sections of a text. You'll never improve unless you have the confidence to move on. Try covering the text you've just read with a piece of paper. And to prove to yourself that you *have* actually understood, summarise in a sentence or two what you've read when you get to the end of a page. You'll be surprised by how much you remember.

You will now hear Part 2 again.

This is the end of Part 2.

 **Track 16**

Part 3

You are going to hear five extracts in which people talk about a person they are close to. For questions 19–23, choose from the list A–H the person each speaker describes. Use the letters once only. There are three letters that you do not need to use.
You have 30 seconds to look at Part 3.

Speaker 1

Man: I've got lots of acquaintances but just a couple of people that I class as being special. One of those is Cameron. He's so cheerful that it's guaranteed he'll cheer me up if I'm feeling down. I've known him for years, since we were at school, and we're very close. We have a long shared history so we can talk about things in a way that isn't possible with other people I know.

Speaker 2

Woman: I met Christine ten years ago when I was a nurse, but my opinion of her wasn't very positive at first. She's one of those people who sometimes seem to be uninterested in others. But as we got to know each other, we discovered we enjoyed each other's company. We laugh about the same things and have similar interests. We're the best of friends and even though we work in different hospitals now, we still see each other.

Speaker 3

Man: I left college three years ago and got a job in an accountancy firm, where I shared an office with Jon, who had joined the company the year before. It was my first job and I was scared of making mistakes. But Jon was brilliant and spent hours helping me to learn new systems and processes even though he was busy himself. We became really good friends and see each other regularly outside of work.

Speaker 4

Woman: Without doubt, my closest friend is my husband. I've got my own friends and I love them all but Paul is obviously special. He's so laid-back and patient and rarely gets cross about anything. He even kept calm when he was teaching me to drive! I kept doing things wrong and he just kept telling me not to worry about my mistakes and not to let them affect my confidence.

Speaker 5

Woman: I've known Amanda for years and in fact, she was a bridesmaid at my wedding. But she was very ill recently and had to spend a lengthy period in hospital. I hated seeing her suffer but I'm happy to say she made a full recovery. We both love classical music and now we can go to concerts together again, which is great as my husband isn't interested in that kind of thing.

You will now hear Part 3 again.

This is the end of Part 3.

 **Track 17**

Part 4

You are going to hear part of an interview with a woman called Yvonne, who is a yoga instructor. For questions 24–30, choose the correct answer, A, B or C.
You have one minute to look at Part 4.

Presenter: Yvonne, how did you become interested in yoga?

Yvonne: Soon after I'd given birth to my first child, I started getting back pain and tried everything to treat it, but with no success. Then a friend suggested yoga. I was in so much pain that I didn't need much persuading, and after a few weeks my back felt better. I'd never been a great one for exercise so I was amazed how much I enjoyed it.

Presenter: When did you decide you were going to teach professionally?

Yvonne: About three years ago. I was a school teacher at the time but I decided to go on a part-time contract with my school and run yoga sessions in my spare time at a local sports centre. Then I was offered the chance to rent a room in a leisure centre so I gave up the teaching job to do yoga full time.

Presenter: What's the most rewarding part of your work?

Yvonne: Well, I always enjoyed being a teacher and I get the same satisfaction from being a yoga instructor. I like helping people to discover what interests them. I love seeing people transform from people in physical or emotional pain into positive, healthy individuals. Some become passionate about yoga. I find *that* particularly satisfying.

Presenter: Now what changes would I notice in my physical and mental health if I took up yoga?

Yvonne: It's an excellent means of improving your strength and flexibility and it can help relieve aches and pains. I've also lowered my blood pressure since doing it. It can help people suffering from stress, and lots of clients say their memory and concentration have improved since they've started.

Presenter: Presumably, people notice the benefits of yoga in conjunction with a healthy lifestyle and diet.

Yvonne: Yes. Yoga is about achieving balance and this applies to your life generally. We should take steps to become positive, to avoid people who make us feel bad about ourselves, to see the best in others and be kind.

Presenter: What about diet?

Yvonne: Personally, I eat seasonally and locally. Fresh, locally produced food is likely to be healthier and less expensive. And when we're eating, we should enjoy our food. Don't rush your meals so you can watch TV. And although the odd bar of chocolate or biscuit won't kill you, eat things like that in moderation.

Presenter: What advice would you give to anyone thinking of taking up yoga?

Yvonne: I'd say speak to people who have done it and ask them how they've benefited. Sometimes that's more persuasive than asking an instructor. Find a local school and see if they have introductory sessions. But the most important thing is to give it a chance. Do it for at least three months. Then you'll know for sure whether it's your thing or not.

You will now hear Part 4 again.

This is the end of Part 4.
There will now be a pause of five minutes so that you can copy your answers onto the separate answer sheet. Make sure you follow the numbering of all the questions. I will let you know when there is one minute left.

Sample answer sheets

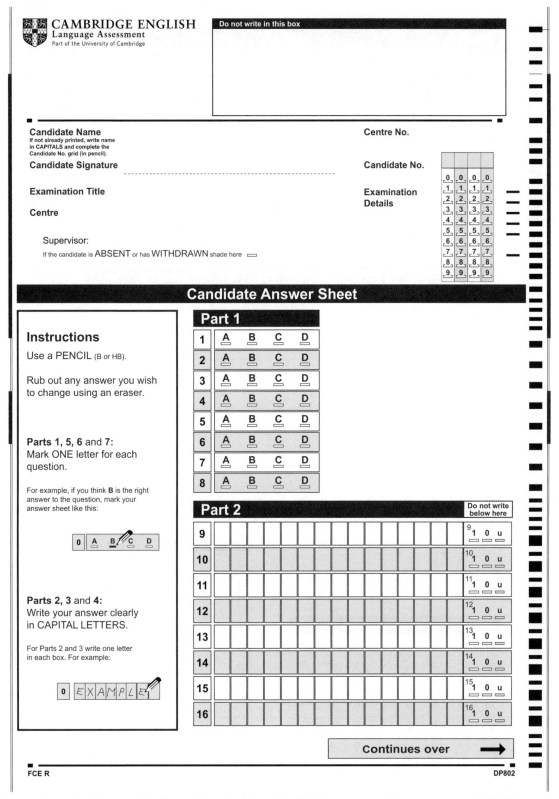

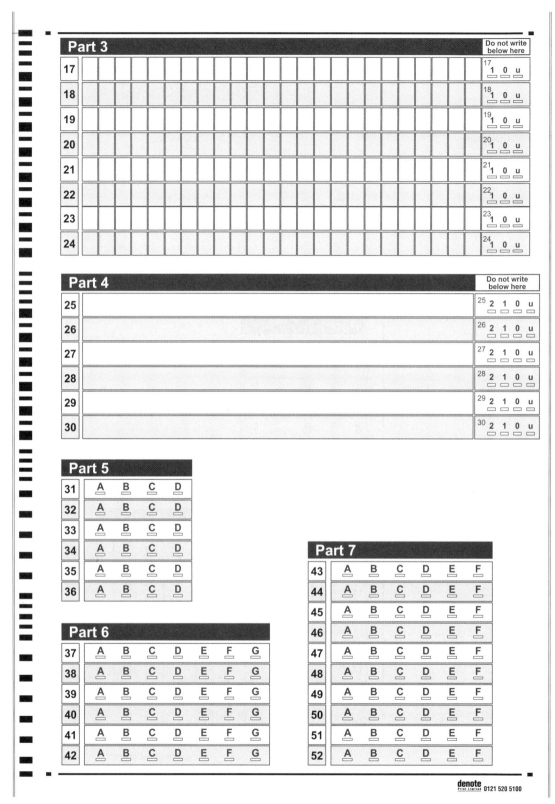

Part 3

																						Do not write below here
17																						17 1 0 u
18																						18 1 0 u
19																						19 1 0 u
20																						20 1 0 u
21																						21 1 0 u
22																						22 1 0 u
23																						23 1 0 u
24																						24 1 0 u

Part 4

	Do not write below here
25	25 2 1 0 u
26	26 2 1 0 u
27	27 2 1 0 u
28	28 2 1 0 u
29	29 2 1 0 u
30	30 2 1 0 u

Part 5

31	A	B	C	D
32	A	B	C	D
33	A	B	C	D
34	A	B	C	D
35	A	B	C	D
36	A	B	C	D

Part 6

37	A	B	C	D	E	F	G
38	A	B	C	D	E	F	G
39	A	B	C	D	E	F	G
40	A	B	C	D	E	F	G
41	A	B	C	D	E	F	G
42	A	B	C	D	E	F	G

Part 7

43	A	B	C	D	E	F
44	A	B	C	D	E	F
45	A	B	C	D	E	F
46	A	B	C	D	E	F
47	A	B	C	D	E	F
48	A	B	C	D	E	F
49	A	B	C	D	E	F
50	A	B	C	D	E	F
51	A	B	C	D	E	F
52	A	B	C	D	E	F

CAMBRIDGE ENGLISH
Language Assessment
Part of the University of Cambridge

Do not write in this box

Candidate Name
If not already printed, write name in CAPITALS and complete the Candidate No. grid (in pencil).

Candidate Signature

Examination Title

Centre

Supervisor:
If the candidate is ABSENT or has WITHDRAWN shade here ⬜

Centre No.

Candidate No.

Examination Details

0 0 0 0
1 1 1 1
2 2 2 2
3 3 3 3
4 4 4 4
5 5 5 5
6 6 6 6
7 7 7 7
8 8 8 8
9 9 9 9

Candidate Answer Sheet

Instructions

Use a PENCIL (B or HB).
Rub out any answer you wish to change using an eraser.

Parts 1, 3 and **4:**
Mark ONE letter for each question.

For example, if you think **B** is the right answer to the question, mark your answer sheet like this:

0 | A | B | C

Part 2:
Write your answer clearly in CAPITAL LETTERS.

Write one letter or number in each box.
If the answer has more than one word, leave one box empty between words.

For example:

0 | A N | E X A M P L E

Turn this sheet over to start.

FCE L   DP799

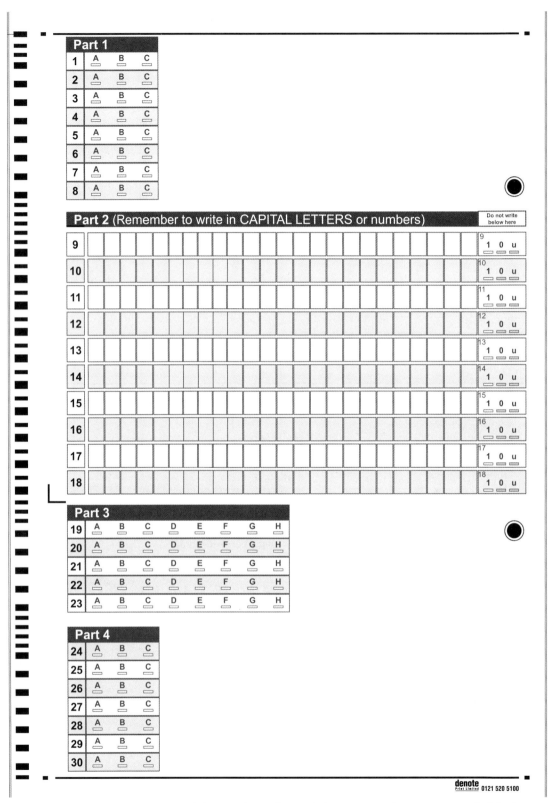

Part 1

	A	B	C
1	⊏⊐	⊏⊐	⊏⊐
2	⊏⊐	⊏⊐	⊏⊐
3	⊏⊐	⊏⊐	⊏⊐
4	⊏⊐	⊏⊐	⊏⊐
5	⊏⊐	⊏⊐	⊏⊐
6	⊏⊐	⊏⊐	⊏⊐
7	⊏⊐	⊏⊐	⊏⊐
8	⊏⊐	⊏⊐	⊏⊐

Part 2 (Remember to write in CAPITAL LETTERS or numbers)

Do not write below here

9	9 1 0 u
10	10 1 0 u
11	11 1 0 u
12	12 1 0 u
13	13 1 0 u
14	14 1 0 u
15	15 1 0 u
16	16 1 0 u
17	17 1 0 u
18	18 1 0 u

Part 3

	A	B	C	D	E	F	G	H
19	⊏⊐	⊏⊐	⊏⊐	⊏⊐	⊏⊐	⊏⊐	⊏⊐	⊏⊐
20	⊏⊐	⊏⊐	⊏⊐	⊏⊐	⊏⊐	⊏⊐	⊏⊐	⊏⊐
21	⊏⊐	⊏⊐	⊏⊐	⊏⊐	⊏⊐	⊏⊐	⊏⊐	⊏⊐
22	⊏⊐	⊏⊐	⊏⊐	⊏⊐	⊏⊐	⊏⊐	⊏⊐	⊏⊐
23	⊏⊐	⊏⊐	⊏⊐	⊏⊐	⊏⊐	⊏⊐	⊏⊐	⊏⊐

Part 4

	A	B	C
24	⊏⊐	⊏⊐	⊏⊐
25	⊏⊐	⊏⊐	⊏⊐
26	⊏⊐	⊏⊐	⊏⊐
27	⊏⊐	⊏⊐	⊏⊐
28	⊏⊐	⊏⊐	⊏⊐
29	⊏⊐	⊏⊐	⊏⊐
30	⊏⊐	⊏⊐	⊏⊐

denote Print Limited 0121 520 5100

CAMBRIDGE ENGLISH
Language Assessment
Part of the University of Cambridge

Do not write in this box

Candidate Name
If not already printed, write name
in CAPITALS and complete the
Candidate No. grid (in pencil).

Centre No.

Candidate No.

Examination Title

Examination
Details

Centre

Supervisor:
If the candidate is ABSENT or has WITHDRAWN shade here ▭

0	0	0	0
1	1	1	1
2	2	2	2
3	3	3	3
4	4	4	4
5	5	5	5
6	6	6	6
7	7	7	7
8	8	8	8
9	9	9	9

Speaking Test Mark Sheet

Date of test:

Month   01 02 03 04 05 06 07 08 09 10 11 12

Day   01 02 03 04 05 06 07 08 09 10 11 12 13 14 15 16 17 18 19 20 21 22 23 24 25 26 27 28 29 30 31

Marks awarded:

	0	1.0	1.5	2.0	2.5	3.0	3.5	4.0	4.5	5.0
Grammar and Vocabulary	0	1.0	1.5	2.0	2.5	3.0	3.5	4.0	4.5	5.0
Discourse Management	0	1.0	1.5	2.0	2.5	3.0	3.5	4.0	4.5	5.0
Pronunciation	0	1.0	1.5	2.0	2.5	3.0	3.5	4.0	4.5	5.0
Interactive Communication	0	1.0	1.5	2.0	2.5	3.0	3.5	4.0	4.5	5.0
Global Achievement	0	1.0	1.5	2.0	2.5	3.0	3.5	4.0	4.5	5.0

Test materials used:

Part 2   1 2 3 4 5 6 7 8 9 10 11 12 13 14 15 16 17 18 19 20

Part 3   21 22 23 24 25 26 27 28 29 30

Assessor's number	Interlocutor's number	Test format	Number of 2nd Candidate	Number of 3rd Candidate
A A 0 0 A A	A A 0 0 A A	Examiners : Candidates	0 0 0 0	0 0 0 0
B B 1 1 B B	B B 1 1 B B		1 1 1 1	1 1 1 1
C C 2 2 C C	C C 2 2 C C		2 2 2 2	2 2 2 2
D D 3 3 D D	D D 3 3 D D	2 : 2	3 3 3 3	3 3 3 3
E E 4 4 E E	E E 4 4 E E		4 4 4 4	4 4 4 4
F F 5 5 F F	F F 5 5 F F	2 : 3	5 5 5 5	5 5 5 5
G G 6 6 G G	G G 6 6 G G		6 6 6 6	6 6 6 6
H H 7 7 H H	H H 7 7 H H		7 7 7 7	7 7 7 7
J J 8 8 J J	J J 8 8 J J		8 8 8 8	8 8 8 8
K K 9 9 K K	K K 9 9 K K		9 9 9 9	9 9 9 9

SMS 1   **denote** Print Limited 0121 520 5100

DP749/307

Reproduced with permission of Cambridge English Language Assessment © 2015

Answer key

TEST 1

Paper 1 Reading and Use of English

Part 1

1	C	4	C	7	D
2	A	5	A	8	B
3	D	6	A		

Part 2

9	between	12	in	15	who
10	the	13	has	16	be
11	which	14	a		

Part 3

17	treatments	21	possibility
18	numerous	22	infection
19	circulation	23	overestimate
20	popularity	24	unhygienic

Part 4

25 far as | I am/I'm concerned
26 an/any interest | in
27 in order | to teach
28 a good idea | to buy
29 get on | with
30 long as | you pay

Part 5

31	C	33	A	35	D
32	B	34	C	36	C

Part 6

37	E	39	F	41	G
38	C	40	A	42	B

Part 7

43	B	47	D	51	A
44	C	48	A	52	C
45	C	49	D		
46	A	50	B		

Paper 3 Listening

Part 1

1	A	4	A	7	C
2	B	5	A	8	B
3	C	6	C		

Part 2

9	(school) playground
10	correct order
11	colour
12	young children
13	different times
14	map
15	mobile phone signal
16	record
17	long trousers
18	introduction

Part 3

19	F	21	E	23	A
20	H	22	C		

Part 4

24	B	28	A
25	C	29	B
26	A	30	C
27	A		

TEST 2

Paper 1 Reading and Use of English

Part 1

1	A	4	C	7	B
2	A	5	C	8	A
3	B	6	D		

Part 2

9	be / make	13	who / that
10	to	14	than
11	were	15	without
12	if / whether	16	may / might / could

Part 3

17	natural	21	pollution
18	inhabitants	22	inefficient
19	security	23	considerations
20	economic	24	protection

Part 4

25 spite of | the bad weather
26 came up | with
27 had not/hadn't seen Mark | for
28 I known | about
29 would/'d sooner | have
30 must have | decided

Part 5

31	A	**34**	C
32	B	**35**	A
33	D	**36**	D

Part 6

37	D	**40**	E
38	G	**41**	B
39	A	**42**	F

Part 7

43	D	**48**	C
44	A	**49**	D
45	B	**50**	B
46	A	**51**	D
47	B	**52**	C

Paper 3 Listening

Part 1

1	C	**4**	B	**7**	C
2	B	**5**	B	**8**	A
3	A	**6**	C		

Part 2

9	(local) library	**14**	social media
10	child's name	**15**	privacy settings
11	bank	**16**	young people
12	bought something	**17**	photos and music
13	wireless networks	**18**	week

Part 3

19	G	**22**	H
20	E	**23**	A
21	C		

Part 4

24	A	**28**	A
25	C	**29**	C
26	B	**30**	A
27	C		

TEST 3

Paper 1 Reading and Use of English

Part 1

1	C	**4**	A	**7**	D
2	D	**5**	D	**8**	C
3	A	**6**	B		

Part 2

9 if / when
10 out
11 what / the
12 that
13 as
14 who / that
15 are
16 than

Part 3

17	employment	**21**	transparency
18	creation	**22**	responsibility
19	population	**23**	privacy
20	knowledge	**24**	disadvantage

Part 4

25 is/'s | no point (in) / is not/isn't any point | in
26 have been held | up
27 was no need | for / was not/wasn't any need | for
28 you ask | me
29 objected to | going
30 had | no idea / did not/didn't have any idea

Part 5

31	D	**33**	D	**35**	B
32	A	**34**	C	**36**	D

Part 6

37	D	**39**	G	**41**	E
38	B	**40**	A	**42**	F

Part 7

43	D	**47**	D	**51**	B
44	B	**48**	A	**52**	A
45	A	**49**	C		
46	C	**50**	B		

Paper 3 Listening

Part 1

1	C	4	B	7	B
2	B	5	B	8	A
3	C	6	A		

Part 2

9 reports
10 promotion
11 excellent service
12 term
13 in full
14 feedback form
15 (college) training days
16 café/cafe
17 team-building/team building
18 catering

Part 3

19	G	21	E	23	A
20	C	22	D		

Part 4

24	B	28	C
25	B	29	B
26	B	30	A
27	C		

TEST 4

Paper 1 Reading and Use of English

Part 1

1	A	5	C
2	D	6	C
3	A	7	D
4	B	8	B

Part 2

9	than	13	all
10	there	14	if / when
11	what	15	it
12	as	16	be

Part 3

17	volcanic	21	conclusion
18	variations	22	effective
19	activity	23	projections
20	involvement	24	shortages

Part 4

25 was not/wasn't possible | for
26 is no truth | in / is not/isn't any truth | in
27 denied that | he/she had cheated /
    denied | cheating/having cheated
28 insisted on | me/my
29 is said | to be
30 goes on | about

Part 5

31	B	33	A	35	B
32	B	34	A	36	C

Part 6

37	E	39	B	41	A
38	G	40	F	42	D

Part 7

43	B	47	C	51	B
44	D	48	A	52	D
45	C	49	C		
46	A	50	D		

Paper 3 Listening

Part 1

1	B	4	A	7	C
2	B	5	C	8	C
3	A	6	B		

Part 2

9 techniques
10 timing
11 out loud
12 pen/finger (tip)
13 (any) meaning
14 houses
15 headings
16 opening
17 confidence
18 summarise

Part 3

19	C	22	H
20	G	23	A
21	F		

Part 4

24	B	28	C
25	A	29	A
26	B	30	C
27	C		

Framework for Paper 4: Speaking

Below there are examples of what the examiner might say in each part of the Speaking paper and the questions he/she might ask. You should become familiar with the 'framework' for the Speaking paper because this will help you to understand the kinds of answers you need to give.

TEST 1

Part 1   (2 minutes)

Examiner: (to Candidates A and B) Good morning/afternoon/evening. My name is ... and this is my colleague ... . And your names are?
Can I have your mark sheets, please?
Thank you.

Examiner: Where are you from, (Candidate A)?
And you, (Candidate B)?
First we'd like to know something about you.
(The examiner asks one or more questions from a number of categories.)

Examiner: (possible questions)

- How do you spend your weekends?

- What's your favourite day of the week?

- Do you watch a lot of TV?

Part 2   (4 minutes)

Examiner: In this part of the test, I'm going to give each of you two photographs.
I'd like you to talk about your photographs on your own for about a minute,
and also to answer a question about your partner's photographs.

(Candidate A), it's your turn first. Here are your photographs. They show
people who are travelling to work.

(The examiner shows the photographs on page ii to Candidate A.)

Examiner: I'd like you to compare the photographs and say **why you think these
people have chosen to travel to work in this way**. All right?

(Candidate A talks for one minute.)
Candidate A: --

Examiner: Thank you. (Candidate B), **how do you prefer to travel to college? Why?**

(Candidate B talks for 30 seconds.)
Candidate B: --

Examiner: Thank you.

Examiner: Now, (Candidate B), here are your photographs. They show **people learning in different ways**.

(The examiner shows the photographs on page iii to Candidate B.)

Examiner: I'd like you to compare the photographs and say **why the teachers have organised their classes in this way.** All right?

(Candidate B talks for one minute.)
Candidate B: --

Examiner: Thank you. (Candidate A), **how do you prefer to learn, and why?**

(Candidate A talks for 30 seconds.)
Candidate A: --

Examiner: Thank you.

Part 3 (4 minutes)

Examiner: Now, I'd like you to talk about something together for about two minutes. **I'd like you to imagine that a school is organising an educational trip for its students. Here some places the school could choose and a question for you to discuss.** First you have some time to look at the task.

(The examiner shows the prompts on page iv to the candidates. He/She allows 15 seconds.)

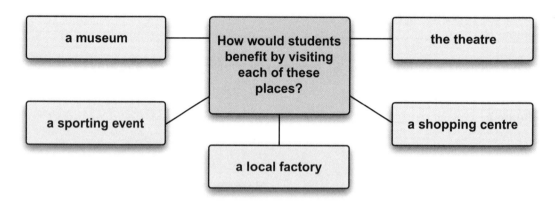

Examiner: Now, talk to each other about **how students would benefit by visiting each of these places.**

(Candidates talk together for two minutes.)
Candidates: --

Examiner: Thank you. Now you have about a minute to decide **which two places would be the best for the students to visit.**

(Candidates talk together for one minute.)
Candidates: --

Examiner: Thank you.

Part 4 (4 minutes)

Examiner:

- Do you think students enjoy school trips?

- Why do you think schools try to organise trips?

- Is it important to include all students in school trips?

Thank you. That is the end of the test.

TEST 2

Part 1   (2 minutes)

Examiner: (to Candidates A and B) Good morning/afternoon/evening. My name is ...
and this is my colleague ... . And your names are?
Can I have your mark sheets, please?
Thank you.

Examiner: Where are you from, (Candidate B)?
And you, (Candidate A)?
First we'd like to know something about you.
(The examiner asks one or more questions from a number of categories.)

Examiner: (possible questions)

• Is your city/home town/village a nice place to live?

• Have you lived there long?

• What do you like to do in your spare time?

Part 2　　(4 minutes)

Examiner: In this part of the test, I'm going to give each of you two photographs. I'd like you to talk about your photographs on your own for about a minute, and also to answer a question about your partner's photographs.

(Candidate A), it's your turn first. Here are your photographs. They show **people who are involved in a conversation**.

(The examiner shows the photographs on page vi to Candidate A.)

Examiner: I'd like you to compare the photographs and say **what you think these people are talking about**. All right?

(Candidate A talks for one minute.)
Candidate A: --

Examiner: Thank you. (Candidate B), **how do you feel about talking to people in these situations? Why?**

(Candidate B talks for 30 seconds.)
Candidate B: --

Examiner: Thank you.

Examiner: Now, (Candidate B), here are your photographs. They show **people shopping in different places.**

(The examiner shows the photographs on page vii to Candidate B.)

Examiner: I'd like you to compare the photographs and say **why people choose to shop in these places.** All right?

(Candidate B talks for one minute.)
Candidate B: --

Examiner: Thank you. (Candidate A), **where do you prefer to shop? Why?**

(Candidate A talks for 30 seconds.)
Candidate A: --

Examiner: Thank you.

Part 3 (4 minutes)

Examiner: Now, I'd like you to talk about something together for about two minutes. **I'd like you to imagine that a friend of yours is planning to do a cookery course. Here are some things you could buy him, and a question for you to discuss.** First you have some time to look at the task.
(The examiner shows the prompts on page viii to the candidates. He/She allows 15 seconds.)

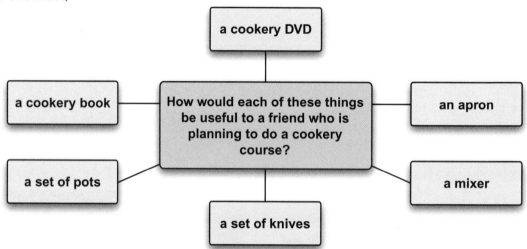

Examiner: Now, talk to each other about **how each of these things would be useful to your friend.**

(Candidates talk together for two minutes.)
Candidates: _____

Examiner: Thank you. Now you have about a minute to decide **which thing would be the best gift.**

(Candidates talk together for one minute.)
Candidates: _____

Examiner: Thank you.

Part 4 (4 minutes)

Examiner:

- Is cookery a popular activity for children?

- Are women better cooks than men?

- Do young people prefer fast food or are they just as interested in eating good quality food?

Thank you. That is the end of the test.

TEST 3

Part 1 (2 minutes)

Examiner: (to Candidates A and B) Good morning/afternoon/evening. My name is ...
and this is my colleague ... . And your names are?
Can I have your mark sheets, please?
Thank you.

Examiner: Where are you from, (Candidate A)?
And you, (Candidate B)?
First we'd like to know something about you.
(The examiner asks one or more questions from a number of categories.)

Examiner: (possible questions)

- How do you like to spend your evenings?

- Do you prefer to spend time on your own or with other people?

- Have you got any hobbies or interests?

Part 2 (2 minutes)

Examiner: In this part of the test, I'm going to give each of you two photographs.
I'd like you to talk about your photographs on your own for about a minute,
and also to answer a question about your partner's photographs.

(Candidate A), it's your turn first. Here are your photographs. They show
people who are waiting to do something.
(The examiner shows the photographs on page x to Candidate A.)

Examiner: I'd like you to compare the photographs and say **what you think these
people are waiting to do.** All right?

(Candidate A talks for one minute.)
Candidate A: --

Examiner: Thank you. (Candidate B), **in which of these situations is it most difficult to
be patient?**

(Candidate B talks for 30 seconds.)
Candidate B: --

Examiner: Thank you.

Examiner: Now, (Candidate B), here are your photographs. They show **people working at home.**

(The examiner shows the photographs on page xi to Candidate B.)

Examiner: I'd like you to compare the photographs and say **why many people choose to do these jobs themselves.** All right?

(Candidate B talks for one minute.)
Candidate B: ---

Examiner: Thank you. (Candidate A), **what jobs do you like doing at home and what jobs don't you like doing?**

(Candidate A talks for 30 seconds.)
Candidate A: ---

Examiner: Thank you.

Part 3   (4 minutes)

Examiner: Now, I'd like you to talk about something together for about two minutes. **I'd like you to imagine that a school wants to show off the talents of its pupils. Here some events it could organise, and a question for you to discuss.** First you have some time to look at the task.

(The examiner shows the prompts on page xii to the candidates. He/She allows 15 seconds.)

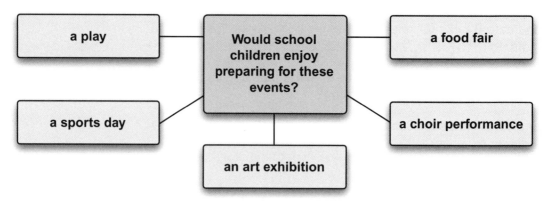

Examiner: Now, talk to each other about **whether school children would enjoy preparing for these events.**

(Candidates talk together for two minutes.)
Candidates: --

Examiner: Thank you. Now you have about a minute to decide **which two events parents would most enjoy attending.**

(Candidates talk together for one minute.)
Candidates: --

Examiner: Thank you.

Part 4   (4 minutes)

Examiner:

• Are children more willing to perform in front of an audience than adults?

• Should we pressurise children to perform if they don't want to?

• Do boys and girls have different preferences when taking part in events like these?

Thank you. That is the end of the test.

TEST 4

Part 1　　(2 minutes)

Examiner: (to Candidates A and B) Good morning/afternoon/evening. My name is ... and this is my colleague ... . And your names are?
Can I have your mark sheets, please?
Thank you.

Examiner: Where are you from, (Candidate A)?
And you, (Candidate B)?
First we'd like to know something about you.
(The examiner asks one or more questions from a number of categories.)

Examiner: (possible questions)

- Do you use the Internet much?

- Do you enjoy reading?

- What's your favourite TV programme?

Part 2   (4 minutes)

Examiner: In this part of the test, I'm going to give each of you two photographs.
I'd like you to talk about your photographs on your own for about a minute,
and also to answer a question about your partner's photographs.

(Candidate A), it's your turn first. Here are your photographs. They show
people taking part in leisure activities.
(The examiner shows the photographs on page xiv to Candidate A.)

Examiner: I'd like you to compare the photographs and say **why people choose to do
activities like these**. All right?

(Candidate A talks for one minute.)
Candidate A: --

Examiner: Thank you. (Candidate B), **which of these activities would you prefer to
do? Why?**

(Candidate B talks for 30 seconds.)
Candidate B: --

Examiner: Thank you.

Examiner: Now, (Candidate B), here are your photographs. They show **people in different parts of the world.**

(The examiner shows the photographs on page xv to Candidate B.)

Examiner: I'd like you to compare the photographs and say **which place you'd prefer to live in.** All right?

(Candidate B talks for one minute.)
Candidate B: --

Examiner: Thank you. (Candidate A), **do you prefer a hot or cold climate?**

(Candidate A talks for 30 seconds.)
Candidate A: --

Examiner: Thank you.

Part 3   (4 minutes)

Examiner: Now, I'd like you to talk about something together for about two minutes. **I'd like you to imagine you are organising a surprise birthday treat for a friend. Here are some things you could do, and a question for you to discuss.** First you have some time to look at the task.

(The examiner shows the prompts on page xvi to the candidates. He/She allows 15 seconds.)

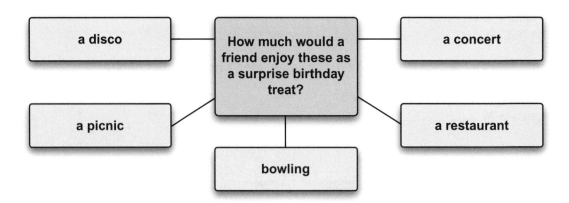

Examiner: Now, talk to each other about **how much your friend would enjoy doing these things.**

(Candidates talk together for two minutes.)
Candidates: --

Examiner: Thank you. Now you have about a minute to decide **which of these things would be the best surprise.**

(Candidates talk together for one minute.)
Candidates: --

Examiner: Thank you.

Part 4   (4 minutes)

Examiner:

- What are some of the difficulties of arranging a surprise like this?

- What events do we tend to remember most clearly when we get older?

- Is it possible to organise a big celebration without spending lots of money?

Thank you. That is the end of the test.

Speaking: model answers

TEST 1

Part 1

18

Examiner:	Good morning. My name is Angela Robinson and this is my colleague, Mark Cooper. And your names are?
Candidate A:	I'm Helmuth Bauer.
Candidate B:	And I'm Brigitte Lefebre.
Examiner:	Can I have your mark sheets, please? Thank you. Now, where are you from, Helmuth?
Candidate A:	I'm from Bielefeld. It's a town in the north of Germany.
Examiner:	And you, Brigitte?
Candidate B:	I come from Paris.
Examiner:	First, we'd like to know something about you. How do you spend your weekends?
Candidate A:	I like to go shopping with my friends. We meet most Saturdays and just walk around the town together.
Examiner:	And you, Brigitte?
Candidate B:	The same, really. I see my friends, sometimes we go to the cinema and I'm also a member of a quiz team. We have a weekly quiz at someone's home every Saturday.
Examiner:	What's your favourite day of the week?
Candidate A:	I think Friday. Yes, Friday at four in the afternoon. That's when college finishes and I know I have the evening and the next two days to relax.
Examiner:	And you, Brigitte?
Candidate B:	For me it's Wednesday. I finish college early on Wednesday afternoons and I go swimming with one of my friends. We both swim for the college team and Wednesday is the day we meet for training. I love it.
Examiner:	Do you watch a lot of TV, Brigitte?
Candidate B:	I'm afraid I do, yes. The TV is often on in my house. I don't watch it all the time – my little sister turns it on when she gets up. I usually ignore it but in the evenings, yes, I watch it quite a lot.
Examiner:	What kind of TV programmes do you like to watch, Helmuth?
Candidate A:	I like films and I watch a lot of dramas ... and reality TV shows. I always say I won't watch them but I do. I like sport too.

Part 2

19

(Candidate A photographs: page ii)
(Candidate B photographs: page iii)

Examiner:	In this part of the test, I'm going to give each of you two photographs. I'd like you to talk about your photographs on your own for about a minute, and also to answer a question about your partner's photographs. Helmuth, it's your turn first. Here are your photographs. They show people who are travelling to work. I'd like you to compare the photographs and say why you think these people have chosen to travel to work in this way. All right?

Candidate A:	In the first photo we can see people taking the train. It doesn't look busy – there are only three people so I don't think it's the rush hour. The man in the foreground is using a laptop, and just behind him is a woman talking on the phone. The second photo shows a man cycling to work. Again, it's quiet and he's the only person on the road, or maybe it's a wide path – there's a park on his left. Now, why are they travelling in this way … Maybe the man on the train has a long journey so *has to* use the train. He can also work while he's travelling, which is useful. The man on the bike can't do any work like that but if there isn't a lot of traffic, cycling can be relaxing. Plus he's keeping fit and saving money.
Examiner:	Thank you. Brigitte, how do you prefer to travel to college and why?
Candidate B:	I prefer to travel by train if I'm going to college, like the man in the photo. If I'm very lucky, I get a seat. Then it's a chance to do some work, or read, or study or just relax before I get there. The roads in Paris are very busy so cycling isn't safe. And I haven't got a driving licence or a car.
Examiner:	Thank you. Now, Brigitte, here are your photographs. They show people learning in different ways. I'd like you to compare the photographs and say why the teachers have organised their classes in this way. All right?
Candidate B:	Hmm. Um, well, both photographs were taken in a classroom. This one shows a class of adults all sitting at desks. There's a teacher at the front of the class standing at a whiteboard and explaining something to the students. In the second picture there are three children sitting at a table. They're smiling and they seem to be having fun. We can't see the teacher in this photo but he or she is probably with another group of children in the class. The teacher in the first photo might have some important information to tell the students, just like in a lecture at university. I think this is the best way to give lots of people information. In the second photo the teacher probably wants the children to learn together, to help each other with something, or maybe to discuss something together.
Examiner:	Thank you. Helmuth, how do you prefer to learn, and why?
Candidate A:	Well, like Brigitte said, it depends on the situation. I prefer to be in a lecture like the first photo if I need to find out information – for an essay, for example. But always being in a lecture is a bit boring. Sometimes it's enjoyable to share your opinions with others or try to solve a problem in a group.
Examiner:	Thank you.

Part 3

(Visual materials: page iv)

Examiner:	Now, I'd like you to talk about something together for about two minutes. I'd like you to imagine that a school is organising an educational trip for its students. Here are some places the school could choose, and a question for you to discuss. First, you have some time to look at the task. Now, talk to each other about how students would benefit by visiting each of these places.
Candidate A:	OK, shall I start? I think all these places are common for school trips, aren't they? What do you think about an education trip to a museum?
Candidate B:	Yes, museums are OK – if you're doing a History project, for example, or there's an interesting exhibition. You can learn a lot from a short visit. But the factory would be interesting as well. People don't often get the chance to see how things are made – not very often, anyway. That would be good.

Candidate A: That's true. I went on a trip to a factory in my country, a car factory, and it was *really* interesting. Now ... the theatre. If you like watching plays, it would be enjoyable, yes? Especially if you're studying the play at school or the theme of the play is very important. Er, what about a sporting event?

Candidate B: Hmm. It depends on the sport, I think. Some students find sport boring and wouldn't really enjoy it. But it can also be good to see people in competition. However, I'm not sure that it's *educational*.

Candidate A: Hmm. What do you think of a shopping centre? I'm sure students would enjoy walking around the shops instead of being in class, but is *that* educational?

Candidate B: Well, maybe the students are studying business. Maybe they have to interview people who own shops or some of the customers. That would be a good way to learn about some things about business.

Candidate A: Yes, that's true.

Examiner: Thank you. Now you have about a minute to decide which two places would be the best for the students to visit.

Candidate B: Do you think the museum might be a bit boring? Schools always take students to museums, don't they?

Candidate A: Yes. I wouldn't choose the museum ... And the theatre ... I'm not sure about that. If you're studying the play, it would be useful but if you're not, it might be boring.

Candidate B: Yes, I agree. I think the factory would be a really good trip and it would appeal to most students. What do you think?

Candidate A: Definitely, yes. Shall we say that's one of our choices? And the shopping centre ... That *could* be good if it's to do with their studies. Better than the sporting event, I think.

Candidate B: OK, now let's choose: the shopping centre or the theatre? Which one's best? Personally, I think if they're related to what the students are studying, the play is best. It can really help you to understand a story or theme better than just reading about it.

Candidate A: Yes, I agree. So that's the factory and the theatre. They're our two choices.

Examiner: Thank you.

Part 4

Examiner: Do you think students enjoy school trips?

Candidate A: Yes, I'm sure they do. Most students would agree that it's a very good idea to get out of the classroom sometimes, and as we said before, it can be a good way to learn about things in a practical way. I know I enjoyed school trips when I was at school. They were a pleasant change from our usual routine.

Examiner: Do you agree, Brigitte?

Candidate B: Yes, I do. I think Helmuth is absolutely right. When I was at school, my classmates and I also loved going on trips and we always looked forward to them. The only problem was that some students couldn't afford to go on some of the trips. You see, my school sometimes organised trips to other countries and they were quite expensive. There was the cost of travelling, accommodation, meals, pocket money ... This meant that the students who couldn't go were left behind – and they felt bad, of course. And the students who could go felt guilty about the ones who couldn't go. But normal trips ... Yes, I think they're an excellent idea.

Examiner: Why do you think schools try to organise trips?

Candidate A:	Well, there are many reasons for this. Sometimes you have to see things, to experience them in real life to understand them. For example, as we said before, if you are studying a play, you have only the words the actors speak in a book. But a play is more than that: it's actions, and lights, and ... lots of other things. So a trip to the theatre is a great opportunity to experience the real play on a stage, a performance. And of course, it's also enjoyable, and it's a great evening out.
Candidate B:	That's right! The students and the teacher can relax together. It's good for everyone in many ways. And trips to other kinds of places give students the chance to see what the things they learn about in class, in theory, are really like. For example, if you are studying, um, lakes ... yes, lakes, in Geography, a trip to a lake can teach you a lot. And if you have a trip to a factory or some other place like that, you can see how it works and maybe talk to the people there and get an idea of what it's really like to work there. So like the business studies example we talked about before, you can learn a lot by going on school trips.
Candidate B:	Yes. If you only learn in class, it's sometimes difficult to understand the subject. In fact, you can get the wrong idea about things. Going on trips can make things clearer.
Examiner:	How important is it to include all students in school trips?
Candidate B:	It's extremely important, like I said before, but it might be difficult to include everybody. In my school we had a trip to Russia for the History students and I remember it cost a lot of money. We went by plane, you see, and stayed in a hotel. Only some students could go.
Candidate A:	I don't think that's good. If the trip is important and helps you to understand a subject better, then everyone should be able to go, not just the students who can afford it. Maybe schools shouldn't choose expensive places. Or maybe the school should organise fundraising events so that all the students can go.
Candidate B:	Yes, or maybe they could have the trip during the holidays. I don't think it's fair if there's a trip and half the class can go somewhere and the other half have to stay in school.
Examiner:	Thank you. That is the end of the test.

TEST 2

Part 1

🎧
22

Examiner:	Good evening. My name is Mark Cooper and this is my colleague, Angela Robinson. And your names are?
Candidate A:	I'm Masako Takahashi.
Candidate B:	And I'm Felipe Álvarez.
Examiner:	Can I have your mark sheets, please? Thank you. Now, where are you from, Felipe?
Candidate B:	I'm from Madrid.
Examiner:	And you, Masako?
Candidate A:	I'm from Seika. It's a town in the prefecture of Kyoto.
Examiner:	First, we'd like to know something about you. Is Seika a nice place to live, Masako?
Candidate A:	Yes, I love living there. We have lots of festivals during the year and recently a large science park was built there – there's lots to do.

Examiner:	And you, Felipe?
Candidate B:	Yes, I like living in Madrid. I enjoy being in a busy city as there's lots to do. And I think Madrid is a beautiful city as well.
Examiner:	Have you lived there long, Felipe?
Candidate B:	Yes, I have. I was born in Madrid and my mother and father come from Madrid too. I don't think I'd like to live anywhere else.
Examiner:	And you, Masako?
Candidate A:	Yes. I've also always lived in Seiko so I can't imagine living anywhere else. Maybe I will have to, though, if I need to get a job in another place, like Tokyo.
Examiner:	What do you like to do in your spare time, Masako?
Candidate A:	I play the piano and I spend a lot of time practising. We have a piano at home but I also go to classes. I like to see my friends, of course. We often go out to the shops together or to the cinema.
Examiner:	And you, Felipe?
Candidate B:	I go out with my friends as well. There's always so much to do in Madrid – like any big city, really. I also love football and I'm in a team. We play matches most Sundays and train on Wednesday and Friday evenings.

Part 2

🎧 23

(Candidate A photographs: page vi)
(Candidate B photographs: page vii)

Examiner:	In this part of the test, I'm going to give each of you two photographs. I'd like you to talk about your photographs on your own for about a minute, and also to answer a question about your partner's photographs. Masako, it's your turn first. Here are your photographs. They show people who are involved in a conversation. I'd like you to compare the photographs and say what you think these people are talking about. All right?
Candidate A:	OK ... Yes ... There are people involved in a conversation in both these scenes but in completely different situations. In the first photo we can see a group of friends, they're probably two couples. There are two men and two women and they look like they're having fun. I imagine they're in a café as they have drinks. They look like they're laughing at a joke. It's much more fun than the second scene. They're wearing casual clothes and relaxing. The other photograph shows a group of people in a business meeting. They're sitting around a table in a modern office and they're probably discussing business issues. Again, there are two women and two men. One of the women is smiling, and the man on the left looks relaxed. In fact, everyone looks quite relaxed. All four people are wearing suits and they're probably discussing something more serious than the first group of people.
Examiner:	Thank you. Felipe, how do you feel about talking to people in these situations, and why?
Candidate B:	Well, I don't have a job yet so I don't know what it feels like to be in a business meeting. I imagine it's very interesting to discuss things or try to solve problems with your colleagues. But I think I prefer talking with my friends and relaxing, like the people in the first photo.
Examiner:	Thank you. Now, Felipe, here are your photographs. They show people shopping in different places. I'd like you to compare the photographs and say why people choose to shop in these places. All right?

Candidate B: Well, we can see different ways of shopping in these two photographs. Starting with the photo here, this shows a typical scene in a supermarket. There's a woman with a trolley – I think that's the right word. Anyway, she has one of those and she's deciding what to buy next. The other photograph shows a market. The stall at the front seems to be selling fruit and vegetables and there are other stalls in the background. There are a lot of people in this scene compared to the supermarket. I can only see the woman in the supermarket photo but this isn't typical – supermarkets are usually very busy. This is because people can get all their weekly shopping from there in one trip. You put your shopping in the car and drive home – it's easy. But I think people enjoy markets more. I don't really know why, but most people would say they don't enjoy going to the supermarket. It's just something you have to do. But a market is much more interesting. You don't know what you might find there.

Examiner: Thank you. Masako, where do you prefer to shop, and why?

Candidate A: I agree with Felipe. If I need to get my shopping for the week, it's better to go to a supermarket. It's quick and easy and I prefer to go there for that reason. But if I have more time, then yes, I'd say the market because it's fun to look at the different things people sell there.

Examiner: Thank you.

Part 3

🎧
24

(Visual materials: page viii)

Examiner: Now, I'd like you to talk about something together for about two minutes. I'd like you to imagine that a friend of yours is planning to do a cookery course. Here are some things you could buy him, and a question for you to discuss. First, you have some time to look at the task. Now, talk to each other about how each of these things would be useful to your friend.

Candidate A: Well, all these things are useful if you're learning to cook, aren't they? Especially the cookery book.

Candidate B: Yes, it is. If you're learning, you have to know what ingredients you need and the instructions so a cookery book would be good for a beginner. But actually, I think the DVD is even better if you want to learn how to do something. Don't you agree?

Candidate A: Definitely, yes. Seeing somebody do something is much easier than just reading about how to do it. Now, the knives. It's really important to have a good set of knives if you're preparing food. I read once that if your knives aren't sharp, there's more chance that you'll cut yourself.

Candidate B: That's true. As for the apron, I'm not sure it's important. Our friend might not want to wear one. And I'm not sure people wear aprons when they cook, do they?

Candidate A: Actually, you're wrong. An apron keeps your clothes clean when you're cooking.

Candidate B: I suppose you're right.

Candidate A: Mm. The pots are useful, don't you think? They're very important. But I just thought of something: most people have pots at home so maybe they *aren't* so useful. Maybe the mixer would be more useful: preparing food is much easier with one.

Candidate B: Yes, I agree.

Examiner: Thank you. Now you have about a minute to decide which thing would be the best gift.

Candidate B: Shall we agree that the apron isn't very useful? It would be the cheapest present to buy but probably not the best.

Candidate A: No, I wouldn't buy the apron either, and we agreed that the pots might not be a good idea. He probably already has something he uses to cook things in so let's forget those as well. What about the book or the DVD?

Candidate B: I think both of those would be good. It depends how much money we want to spend, doesn't it? I think he'd love a really good set of knives but they're expensive.

Candidate A: Very expensive, yes. And the mixer might be expensive, although you can get cheap ones. Shall we forget about the money and just say what would be the best gift?

Candidate B: Yes, good idea. In that case, I think the knives would be great – as long as they're very good quality.

Candidate A: Yes. Let's agree on the knives then.

Examiner: Thank you.

Part 4

Examiner: Is cookery a popular activity for children?

Candidate A: Well, I'm not sure it's popular with all children. I think maybe it depends on the age. Young children, when they are four, or five, or six or even a little older, they love mixing things and cooking. I know that my little brother and sister love spending time in the kitchen making cakes and biscuits with my grandmother. The kitchen is a mess afterwards, of course, and there's flour and sugar and eggs and things everywhere, but my grandmother doesn't mind. And it's a fun way for young children to spend an afternoon. And they're very proud when you eat the cakes and biscuits they have made and tell them they taste delicious.

Examiner: Do you agree, Felipe?

Candidate B: Yes, I do. I used to help my grandmother to make bread when I was small. I also enjoyed helping my dad to make lunch on Sundays. In fact, I learnt quite a lot about cooking when I was still very young, only nine or ten. But I think most children, when they get older, they become less interested in cooking. They start to enjoy different things and they think cooking is something adult people do. But cooking is something we can all enjoy at any age if we can make something really delicious or something we haven't tried before but we look forward to eating it.

Examiner: Are women better cooks than men?

Candidate B: That's an interesting question. In my country there are lots of cookery programmes on TV and well-known cooks appear in them, and most of the cooks are men.

Candidate A: Yes, but I don't think this means men are better at cooking than women. I know that another word for a cook is a chef. A chef is a professional cook and most chefs on TV *are* men. It's the same in my country. But I don't think men chefs are better at cooking than women chefs. I think this depends on the person. Some people are good cooks and some people aren't such good cooks, but this has nothing to do with being a man or a woman. I think that if you enjoy cooking and if you do it a lot, and experiment, and try new recipes and get experience, you can become a good cook. Also, in most families in my country, the people who cook the meals are the mothers and the grandmothers.

Examiner:	Do young people prefer fast food or are they just as interested in eating good quality food?
Candidate B:	I think it depends on their parents. If children are used to eating good quality food at home, if their parents cook them delicious meals, I think they'll be used to eating such food and they will probably prefer it to fast food. But most young people like eating fast food sometimes and ... I admit ... I like eating it occasionally when I go out with my friends.
Candidate A:	I eat fast food sometimes, too, but my mum's a very good cook and I look forward to my meals at home more. The taste is better and I feel better after the meal. But a few of my friends eat mainly fast food at home. They order pizzas from takeaways, hamburgers, chips, things like that. I don't understand how they do it. I'd feel sick if I ate food like that every day. So definitely, I agree with Felipe. It depends on the parents and how young people eat at home.
Examiner:	Thank you. That is the end of the test.

TEST 3

Part 1

26

Examiner:	Good afternoon. My name is Adam Thomson and this is my colleague, Elizabeth Gower. And your names are?
Candidate A:	I'm Rosanna Spinella.
Candidate B:	And I'm Evren Çelik.
Examiner:	Can I have your mark sheets, please? Thank you. Now, where are you from, Rosanna?
Candidate A:	I'm from Naples in Italy.
Examiner:	And you, Evren?
Candidate B:	I come from Izmir, in Turkey.
Examiner:	First, we'd like to know something about you. How do you like to spend your evenings Rosanna?
Candidate A:	It depends. During the week, when I have college the next day, I usually stay at home, watch TV, study. But at the weekend I sometimes visit my friends.
Examiner:	And you, Evren?
Candidate B:	I go to evening classes three times a week to study English. On the other nights I stay at home or see my friends.
Examiner:	Do you prefer to spend time on your own or with other people?
Candidate B:	I enjoy both, really. It depends how I'm feeling at the time. Sometimes it's nice to be on your own and relax, especially if you've been busy. But at other times I like to have company and to talk about things with friends.
Examiner:	And you, Rosanna?
Candidate A:	The same, really. I'm with people all day long at college and when I get home, my two younger brothers always want to talk or play so sometimes it's nice to go to my room to be on my own.
Examiner:	Have you got any hobbies or interests?
Candidate A:	Not really, no. I sometimes like to draw or paint but it's not really a *hobby*. I suppose listening to music is a hobby, and I enjoy going to concerts. So let's say that's my interest.

Examiner: And you, Evren?
Candidate B: I'm keen on photography. I saved up for a very long time for a good camera and finally bought one last year. I'm a member of a photography club, which is good fun.

Part 2

(Candidate A photographs: page x)
(Candidate B photographs: page xi)

Examiner: In this part of the test, I'm going to give each of you two photographs. I'd like you to talk about your photographs on your own for about a minute, and also to answer a question about your partner's photographs. Rosanna, it's your turn first. Here are your photographs. They show people who are waiting for something. I'd like you to compare the photographs and say what you think these people are waiting to do. All right?

Candidate A: Right. These photographs show people waiting for things to happen. In the first photo I think they're feeling excited. There's a mother and her two children waiting at the airport. I think they've already checked in and gone through passport control because it looks like they're waiting to board a plane. On the left you can see the aircraft through a big window. Because the woman has her children with her, I think they're going on holiday. Hmm, the other photo shows a group of people in a waiting room. I think it's a doctor's waiting room or maybe they're in a hospital. There are five people in the room. There are two elderly people nearest the camera, a man and a woman, and the woman looks like she has a cold. They might be a couple but I don't think any of the other people know each other as nobody's talking. They're probably feeling ill and need to see the doctor for some medicine. They're just waiting for their name to be called.

Examiner: Thank you. Evren, in which of these situations is it most difficult to be patient?
Candidate B: Definitely the second situation, in a waiting room like this one. If you're at an airport because you're going away on holiday, you feel excited about your flight and so you don't mind the wait. But at the doctor's surgery, you probably feel ill and just want to see the doctor and get home quickly.

Examiner: Thank you. Now, Evren, here are your photographs. They show people working at home. I'd like you to compare the photographs and say why many people choose to do these jobs themselves. All right?

Candidate B: The photographs show people trying to make their homes look nice. In the first photo we can see two people, a man and a woman. The woman's using white paint to paint a wall. I don't think she's holding a paintbrush. It's one of those things you use to paint walls quickly by rolling it across the wall. The man isn't painting. Perhaps he was painting but now he's resting. The other photograph shows a mother and her daughter working in the garden. They're both sitting on the grass and the mother is showing her little girl how to plant some flowers. I think there are two main reasons why many people do these jobs themselves. To begin with, it saves money and they're the kind of jobs that don't require a lot of skill so anyone can do them. But I think the main reason people do these jobs themselves is because they're fun.

Examiner: Thank you. Rosanna, what jobs do you like doing at home and what jobs don't you like doing?

Candidate A: I like doing the jobs in the photos. Painting and gardening are fun and in a way they're quite creative. But there are lots of other jobs that I have to do that I don't like. I hate washing up and tidying my room, for example. It's so boring.

Examiner: Thank you.

Part 3

(Visual materials: page xii)

Examiner: Now, I'd like you to talk about something together for about two minutes. I'd like you to imagine that a school wants to show off the talents of its pupils. Here are some events it could organise, and a question for you to discuss. First, you have some time to look at the task. Now, talk to each other about whether school children would enjoy preparing for these events.

Candidate A: These are all common events that schools organise for pupils. I remember we did most of these things at *my* school. Do *you* think children enjoy doing them?

Candidate B: Definitely. I think they'd enjoy doing a play because they can choose who they want to be. The ones who are confident can play the main roles and children who are shyer can play smaller roles or help with other things.

Candidate A: Yes, I agree. Sports days are always good fun as well. The children get the chance to run around and compete against each other. I also think a food fair is a great idea. Young children love to cook, don't they?

Candidate B: The only problem with the food fair is that the boys might not take it seriously. If they're very young children, six or seven years old, both the boys and the girls would love it for sure. But yes, sports days are always popular. What about an art exhibition?

Candidate A: It's an interesting idea but I'm not sure if it's as much fun as the other things we talked about. The choir performance could be good, though. It's great to be able to sing, and if you're shy or if you don't have a good voice, you can always hide at the back of the choir.

Candidate B: Well, *I* was in a choir at school and I really enjoyed it.

Examiner: Thank you. Now you have about a minute to decide which two events parents would most enjoy attending.

Candidate B: OK. We've already said that the art exhibition isn't as much fun as the other things. Shall we cross that one off?

Candidate A: All right. And I'm not sure about the food fair. It would be interesting to see what your child has made but I think parents would prefer to watch their son or daughter doing something – singing or acting would be much more enjoyable for the parents.

Candidate B: Well, we have three events left, then: the sports day, the play and the choir performance. Which one do we think would be the *least* fun for parents? Personally, I think sports days happen every year, anyway. They did at *my* school.

Candidate A: So you think a sports day wouldn't be as interesting as the other two ideas? I agree, actually. If I had children, I'd love to see them singing or performing in a play. Plus I think these activities make children more confident.

Candidate B: Yes, I agree. So shall we choose the play and the choir performance?

Candidate A: Yes. I think parents would prefer these events.

Examiner: Thank you.

Part 4

🎧
29

Examiner: Are children more willing to perform in front of an audience than adults?

Candidate A: Hmm. That's a very difficult question to answer. Everybody is different, of course, but in my experience, most very young children love performing in front of an audience, especially if they have to dress up in a costume and put on make-up or a mask. It's like a game for them. And let's not forget, when young children give a performance, it's usually in front of people they know, like their parents, their friends' parents, their teachers, so they know the people in the audience. But I think we start to become shyer as we get older – some people do, anyway. But I think perhaps children probably are more willing to perform in front of an audience than adults.

Examiner: Do you agree, Evren?

Candidate B: I don't know, really. I've never thought about it. I remember when I was at primary school, some kids loved acting in plays and singing in concerts, but others didn't want to act or sing. I was rather shy myself, I remember, and I was too scared to do anything in front of other people. I don't know … Maybe some people are born shy, it's their personality, and it doesn't matter if they are children or adults.

Examiner: Should we pressurise children to perform if they don't want to?

Candidate B: I think this is a really important question. If a shy child tells you that he or she doesn't want to perform, it's easy to say 'Oh, all right, you don't have to do it' and choose someone else. But I don't think that helps the shy child at all. It didn't help me when I was in primary school. But then I had a music teacher in high school who … um, encouraged me – I think that's the word – to perform in a school concert. I was very nervous, but the performance went well. I must say, I was surprised and happy when the people in the audience clapped and afterwards they told me I was talented. This gave me more lots more confidence for the next concert and slowly I started to enjoy performing.

Candidate A: I totally agree. I think a teacher should try to encourage children – not force them to sing the song by themselves, or to have a big role in a play. They should be kind and understanding, and get them to do something not so frightening. Even if a child does something small, it will help them to become more confident. And if they are singing with other people in a choir, for example, and make a mistake, it won't be a big problem. They won't be embarrassed.

Examiner: Do boys and girls have different preferences when taking part in events like these?

Candidate B: Um, I don't think it makes any difference when the children are young. When we discussed cooking earlier, we said that boys enjoy it as much as girls but I think this changes when children get older. Boys and girls start to have different preferences. I don't know why.

Candidate A: I'm not sure I agree completely with you, Evren. I think all young children enjoy the same things on the whole. Then, as they get older, some prefer painting and drawing to doing a sport, others prefer acting in a play to cooking, etcetera. But I don't think that's got anything to do with being a boy or a girl. I just think it's to do with what kind of person you are and what things you can do well.

Examiner: Thank you. That is the end of the test.

TEST 4

Part 1

30

Examiner:	Good morning. My name is Elizabeth Gower and this is my colleague, Adam Thomson. And your names are?
Candidate A:	My name is Anna Cabrera.
Candidate B:	And I'm Markus Kleiber.
Examiner:	Can I have your mark sheets, please? Thank you. Now, where are you from, Anna?
Candidate A:	I'm from Barcelona ... well ... a small village just outside the city.
Examiner:	And you, Markus?
Candidate B:	I'm from Munich, in Germany.
Examiner:	First, we'd like to know something about you. Do you use the Internet much, Anna?
Candidate A:	Yes, I use it quite a lot. In fact, since I've had a smartphone I probably use it more than ever.
Examiner:	And you, Markus?
Candidate B:	Yes, me too. I've been using it a lot lately to prepare for this exam – there are lots of websites to help you to practise English.
Examiner:	Do you enjoy reading?
Candidate B:	I'm not very keen on reading literature. I sometimes buy novels but I never seem to find time to read them. But I read a lot of online newspapers and blogs.
Examiner:	And you, Anna?
Candidate A:	I love reading. I usually read two or three books at the same time. My parents think it's funny that I read even while I'm brushing my teeth.
Examiner:	What's your favourite TV programme, Anna?
Candidate A:	I'm keen on documentaries, especially anything about history. I find it easy to remember things I watch on TV compared to just reading about the subject.
Examiner:	And you, Markus?
Candidate B:	I watch a lot of sport like football and rugby, and I'm a big cycling fan so I always watch any events that are on – like the Tour de France.

Part 2

31

(Candidate A photographs: page xiv)
(Candidate B photographs: page xv)

Examiner:	In this part of the test, I'm going to give each of you two photographs. I'd like you to talk about your photographs on your own for about a minute, and also to answer a question about your partner's photographs. Anna, it's your turn first. Here are your photographs. They show people taking part in leisure activities. I'd like you to compare the photographs and say why people choose to do activities like these. All right?
Candidate A:	The first photo shows people walking and the second shows people jogging – in two completely different environments. The first photo has been taken outside. It looks like quite a hot place as the ground looks dry. There's a group of people walking along a wide path with lots of stones and rocks. They're walking away from the camera. On their left is a forest or wood. In fact, it looks like trees have

been cut down to make the path. The people are going towards a rocky hill in the distance. In the second photo we can see a man and a woman on running machines. People walk and jog in places like the ones in the photos to get fit. But in addition to keeping fit, the people in the first photo can also enjoy being in the countryside. I suppose this kind of activity needs to be planned – like a short holiday – whereas a visit to the gym is much easier.

Examiner: Thank you. Markus, which of these activities would you prefer to do, and why?

Candidate B: Well, I'd much sooner be walking out of doors like the people in the first photograph. You benefit from the fresh air, you can look at the scenery – it's fun. But I actually find going to a gym very, very boring. I know it's important to keep fit but I really prefer to keep fit while doing something enjoyable.

Examiner: Thank you. Now, Markus, here are your photographs. They show people in different parts of the world. I'd like you to compare the photographs and say which place you'd prefer to live in. All right?

Candidate B: OK. It's difficult to know exactly where these two places are but the most obvious difference between them is the weather. In the first photo a man is clearing snow from outside his house. It's quite a big house. In fact, the place could be a farm as there are two buildings next to each other and there seems to be a lot of countryside behind the buildings. It's probably very cold and the snow seems to be deep so the man is wearing a hat and gloves. The second photo was probably taken in a country in Africa, and we can see a group of people walking along a path. They're passing some buildings which could be a group of shops in a village. It appears to be very hot as the ground looks dry. Now, I really don't like the cold weather so I wouldn't want to live somewhere that gets lots of snow but I'm also not sure I'd like to live somewhere like the place in the second photograph either. It looks too hot for me and there doesn't seem to be much to do there. If I had to choose, I would probably pick the first place.

Examiner: Thank you. Anna, do you prefer hot or cold climates? And why?

Candidate A: I agree with Markus. I don't like it too hot or too cold so I wouldn't like to live in either of these places. I actually prefer somewhere like the UK, where the weather is average – most of the time!

Examiner: Thank you.

Part 3

(Visual materials: page xvi)

Examiner: Now, I'd like you to talk about something together for about two minutes. I'd like you to imagine you are organising a surprise birthday treat for a friend. Here are some things you could do, and a question for you to discuss. First you have some time to look at the task. Now, talk to each other about how much your friend would enjoy doing these things.

Candidate A: All of these things would be very easy to organise so it's really about whether she – let's say 'she' – would enjoy them. Going to a restaurant is not very exciting or original but if we went to a restaurant that serves the kind of food she likes, she'd find it enjoyable, I think.

Candidate B: Yes. I actually like the idea of the restaurant best of all. A concert is also OK and if we could find out what kind of music she likes and if there are any good concerts around her birthday, she'd have a lovely time. Do you agree?

Candidate A: Yes, I do. Bowling ... It's impossible to say whether she'd enjoy bowling but every time I've been with my friends, we've ended up laughing a lot. And it doesn't matter if you aren't good at it. It's still good fun. That could be a good choice.

Candidate B: That's true. The picnic is also a nice idea but you need to have good weather or it could be a terrible disappointment – and you don't really hear of surprise picnics, do you?

Candidate A: No, you don't. Anyway, she *might* enjoy it but maybe she's like me. I'm not a big fan of picnics and I probably wouldn't pick it for that reason. But it would be easy to arrange a surprise party in a disco and it would mean the party could go on until late, depending on the time the disco closes.

Candidate B: Yes, I hadn't thought of that. And our friend would really love that.

Examiner: Thank you. Now, you have about a minute to decide which of these things would be the best surprise.

Candidate B: OK. I think if we were listening to a band at a concert, we wouldn't be paying attention to our friend so I don't really like the idea of a concert as a surprise, plus it would be difficult to know at what point you would let her know the surprise – outside the concert hall? Inside?

Candidate A: Yes, I see what you mean. The disco would be fun but I'm not sure how you could make it a *surprise*. It would be packed with other people when she arrived and we wouldn't be able to welcome her in the same way as in a restaurant, for example.

Candidate B: What about the restaurant, then? I can imagine one person arranging to go to the restaurant with her and then everyone else could be waiting there for them.

Candidate A: Yes, I think that would be a lovely surprise. I don't think a picnic would be that good. You usually have a picnic in the countryside or in a park and I think it would be hard to think of a reason for taking our friend to a place like that.

Candidate B: Yes, I agree, so it looks like the restaurant or bowling. What do you think of bowling as an idea?

Candidate A: I think bowling would be a great surprise but I like the idea of a meal in a restaurant most of all.

Candidate B: OK, so let's choose the restaurant as the best surprise.

Examiner: Thank you.

Part 4

33

Examiner: What are some of the difficulties of arranging a surprise like this?

Candidate A: Well, there are two main things, really, I think. First of all, you have to choose a place that you can take the person to without them becoming suspicious that something is going on. I mean, it's their birthday so they probably expect to do something special to celebrate on that day. And the second thing is thinking of a place where you can make a booking. It would be terrible to arrive somewhere and then find out that you can't get inside because it's full!

Examiner: Do you agree, Markus?

Candidate B: Yes, I do. Anna is right, but I think there are other difficulties as well. You have to know the person very, very well so that you can arrange a surprise that you are sure they will enjoy. Another thing: you *must* make sure that nobody gives away the surprise. That's difficult because a lot of people can't keep a secret! And of course, you must find out if the person will be available on the day and at the time you've arranged the surprise. You'd need to make *absolutely* sure they hadn't arranged anything else – and I'm not sure how you could do that.

Examiner:	What events do we tend to remember most clearly when we get older?
Candidate B:	Hmm. I think perhaps the events that make us feel emotional make the strongest memories. If you spend a happy time with good friends in a nice place, I'm sure that would be something you wouldn't forget for a long time.
Candidate A:	Yes, I think you're right, Markus. If I think about the things I've done in the past, the ones that I remember the best are the things I did with my friends – the parties I've been to or nice meals in a restaurant. But of course, we also remember very sad times as well. I'll always remember the day our old dog Loco died. I was only five, but it broke my heart. I loved that dog so much. I cried for days. I'll never forget that.
Candidate B:	That's very sad. And what you say is true. We *do* remember the very sad times and we also remember the really important events in our life. For example, our last day at school, the day we meet our future husband or wife, things like that.
Candidate A:	And I also think you remember the things you did that you are proud of and the things you aren't proud of – the things you are sorry you did because they were wrong or bad.
Examiner:	Is it possible to organise a big celebration without spending lots of money?
Candidate B:	I think so. For example, most of the ideas that we spoke about before aren't expensive. The people at a celebration could all do something: some people could make the food, others could bring drinks, others could make decorations, things like that. And if you use your imagination, you can make the celebration really special without spending a lot of money. You could have the celebration on a beautiful beach, or you could organise a street party with your neighbours, or you could have a party with a theme.
Candidate A:	Yes. And the most important thing about a celebration, big or small, is that friends and family celebrate together, have a good time together. It doesn't cost anything to be happy because you're with the people you love.
Examiner:	Thank you. That is the end of the test.

Writing: model answers

TEST 1

Question 1

Students of English know that it takes a lot of work to reach a high level and most people would say that studying in an English-speaking country can be very beneficial. However, for some people, the costs involved in doing this can outweigh the benefits.

The obvious and most significant advantage is that your English is likely to improve more quickly if you are immersed in the language. In addition, you will also have the chance to experience the culture of the host country, which is an important aspect of learning a language. Unfortunately, the costs of studying abroad are out of the reach of many people. Compared to studying in your own country, this option would prove very expensive.

Clearly, time spent in an English-speaking country helps language development but the practicalities of doing so are too expensive for many people. Perhaps one solution is to spend time working in the country instead. This would offer you the chance to learn English in a realistic setting but leave open the option of taking a course either at home or abroad.

Question 2

I have several pleasant memories of my time at secondary school. One memory in particular involves my love of football.

As soon as playtime came, my friends and I would all run out to the playground, quickly get into teams and play our daily game of football. We used to take these games very seriously. This was partly because we wanted to win but also because we didn't know if the sports teacher was watching. Maybe one of us would get picked for the school team!

Then one day it happened. After a sports lesson the teacher called me over and asked me if I wanted to play for the team the following Saturday. He wasn't promising that I would play but he said I would certainly be a substitute. I felt so proud and excited. I went home and told my parents, who treated me to a new set of boots.

I actually played that Saturday and soon got a regular place in the team. But it's the teacher inviting me to play that is still the fondest memory I have.

Question 3

Hi Chris,

I hope you're well. Many thanks for offering to help me find somewhere to live.

I'll be working in the UK for three months so I'll need somewhere for that period of time. I start my job at the beginning of September. It's only me so I don't need a house or anything too big – just a one-bedroom flat or even a bedsit would be OK. I don't know what the cost of accommodation is like in England but I'd prefer not to have anything too expensive. The company are going to pay the rent but I don't want to spend too much of their money!

It would be great if you could find somewhere near the centre. If I'm close to the office, I won't have to spend a lot of money on bus or train fares and I'll also be able to have a look around the sights. But if you can't find anything in the centre, somewhere in the suburbs will be fine.

Once again, many thanks for offering to help. Write back soon and let me know how you get on.

Lauren

Question 4

Introduction

This report presents staff feedback on the recent staff training day and suggestions for improvements in the future.

The training

Most of the staff who attended the event were happy with the choice of training sessions and enjoyed the day. However, a minority argued that the event should not have been held in the summer as many people were unable to attend because they were away on holiday.

The facilities

The staff who attended were pleased with the quality of the training but there were several complaints about the computer equipment. Some PCs failed to work and there was a long period when the Internet was unavailable. There were also complaints about the size of the rooms, which some people said were too small.

Recommendations

We should not run events during holiday periods when staff are away from work. The winter months or early spring would be better. We should also make sure all the equipment required for the day is working properly. Finally, the rooms used for training should be large enough to cater comfortably for the number of people attending.

TEST 2

Question 1

As well as giving us financial security, having a job is important because it largely defines who we are. For example, the first question we are frequently asked when meeting someone for the first time is: 'What do you do?' However, in difficult economic times there is stiff competition for the few jobs available, particularly between younger and older people.

For young people, their first job is a crucial step in their career. Unless they actually start working, they will never be able to gain the experience employers demand. On the other hand, older people usually have years of experience already and so are more attractive to potential employers. They are also more likely to have family responsibilities and therefore in need of employment.

Despite this, I feel we should give priority to younger people. Without the chance to enter the workplace, they could find themselves facing years of idleness and frustration and they will never get experience to build on in later life. At the same time, I believe companies should implement a quota system to ensure they also employ an acceptable number of older people.

Question 2

St Stephen's Community Carnival is a yearly festival that takes place in a park in the centre of my town. Like other summer fairs and carnivals, it is organised by small businesses, community groups and local institutions, and is a fun day out for the whole family. It is more than just an event for local people to attend, however. A successful festival relies on volunteers to make things run smoothly and it is a chance for people to get involved and meet other like-minded people.

Our town's carnival has suffered in the past few years from bad weather, and heavy rain has kept people away. However, on dry or sunny days the carnival is a great day out. The children can enjoy the entertainment on offer and adults can look around the many stalls selling locally made products or providing information about community groups and local clubs.

Most towns and villages in my country have a similar festival during the summer months. It is a good idea if you are visiting the area to check out the dates of the events as they will provide you with a great day out.

Question 3

> *Hi Emma,*
>
> *I'm so pleased you can come to my party!*
>
> *Getting to my house from the airport is quite simple. There's a train service from there to Broad Street Station in the city centre – it only takes fifteen minutes. I think the trains run every half an hour. From the city centre you can catch a bus to my house – the number 36 in the direction of Coleshill. After about ten stops, you'll come to a big supermarket on your left and a park on the right-hand side of the road. Get off at the supermarket – you'll see my road just past the supermarket – Oxford Road.*
>
> *By the way, remember to buy a day ticket at the airport. You can use it both on the train from the airport and on all local buses – and it doesn't cost too much!*
>
> *As for the weather, it'll be warm so just wear something light. However, we may have a few showers, so you might want to bring an umbrella.*
>
> *Really looking forward to seeing you!*
>
> *Mark*

Question 4

> *Introduction*
>
> *This report looks at the views of local people about the shopping facilities in our area and it also offers suggestions on how they can be improved.*
>
> *Transport*
>
> *The people I spoke to all feel the shopping centre is well served by buses. A frequent complaint, however, was the lack of parking facilities and many said they would be more likely to come into town if this problem could be solved.*
>
> *The shops*
>
> *Most people think there is a good selection of shops. They particularly liked the fact that there are lots of independent shops as well as the usual national chain stores. Some people said they would like to see something done about the busy road that goes through the main shopping area as this affects their shopping experience negatively.*
>
> *Recommendations*
>
> *Local people are happy with the range of shops. The main problem seems to be heavy traffic and a lack of parking spaces. To bring more people into the area, the council should consider creating more parking. In the longer term, planners could consider re-routing some traffic away from the shopping centre.*

TEST 3

Question 1

Whenever you pick up a newspaper or switch on the TV, there seems to be a report explaining how our health is suffering because of poor diet. This problem has become more serious with the growth in the number of fast food restaurants and the consumption of processed ready meals. Experts have different views about how this problem can be addressed.

On the one hand, it is argued that governments should take action. For example, laws could be introduced which limit how much salt can be added to foods. In addition, many health professionals believe that advertisements for fast food aimed at children should be banned. Others feel we should be allowed to make our own decisions about the food we eat and that governments should not interfere in such matters.

Since people have no control over the ingredients in the foods they buy, I feel there should be regulation to deal with this. However, people also need to learn which foods are healthy and how to prepare them healthily and so I think education is the key to improving our diet.

Question 2

Introduction

In order to find out local people's attitudes to crime in the area where I live, I carried out a survey of people leaving my local supermarket.

Types of crime

The people I spoke to thought that burglary and car and mobile phone theft were the most common crimes, followed by vandalism such as graffiti. Approximately half the people I spoke to said they had been victims of crime. Younger people were more concerned about having their phone stolen whilst older people were worried about burglary.

Preventing crime

Most people said they made sure their house was secure and that they always locked doors and windows. Car owners either kept their car in a garage or parked it as close to their home as possible. Young people said they tried not to be too obvious when using their phone.

Lowering the crime rate

The majority of people said that the best way to reduce crime was to take steps to prevent it, such as those listed above. Most felt there should also be more police on the streets and a minority wanted to see tougher punishments for criminals.

Question 3

> *Hi Anna!*
>
> *It was great to hear from you. We're all fine, thanks. Your project sounds very interesting and I'm happy to help.*
>
> *As you know, young people are all different and have their own interests but I think in my country most teenagers love to wander around the shops at the weekend. I also enjoy window shopping with my friends although I don't always buy something! When the weather's nice, we like to go to the park and just sit around talking or playing games. Unfortunately, this doesn't happen very often as it rains a lot in my country.*
>
> *On Saturday evenings a lot of teenagers have a sleepover at one of their friend's homes. I always look forward to these – we all take some snacks with us and choose two or three films to watch. The only problem is we get to sleep very late and feel exhausted the next day. I think most Sunday evenings are spent getting ready for school the next day and doing any homework that needs finishing.*
>
> *I hope this helps. Write back soon!*
>
> *Eva*

Question 4

> *A holiday of a lifetime*
>
> *Some people dream of beautiful beaches on paradise islands. Others imagine taking a cruise to faraway locations. Sadly, I get seasick and find lying on the beach quite boring. So what would I choose to do? Simple! I'd love to spend as much time as possible cycling through one of my favourite countries, Greece.*
>
> *It may sound anti-social but I would definitely prefer to go on my own. On a holiday like this, I'd like to meet and speak with local people. If you don't have a friend with you, the only way to get into conversation is to speak with strangers.*
>
> *I don't know Greece very well so I can't say exactly where I would go. But I'd love to cycle from the north of the country all the way down to Athens. I'd try to use the small roads that go through little towns and villages and I'd be able to live on delicious Greek food.*
>
> *I know cycling through Greece would take longer than a typical two-week holiday but hopefully this won't stop me winning the competition!*

TEST 4

Question 1

It is impossible to imagine a world without advertising. We see adverts on television, as we walk or drive around the streets, in fact everywhere we go. However, is it appropriate to aim adverts at young children?

Children often put pressure on their parents to buy them the things they see advertised. However, most sensible parents do not want to spoil their child. They may also refuse to buy things because quite simply, they can't afford them. This often results in arguments, which are made worse if the child's friends have the desired objects.

On the other hand, children need to learn how to live in a world where advertising plays such an important role. The ability to see through the hype and view media messages critically is an essential skill that children need to develop.

I feel it is important that children learn lessons in life and one of those lessons is how to live in a world dominated by advertising. Rather than banning adverts, perhaps schools could spend time teaching children how to deal with the powerful influence of the advertising industry.

Question 2

Have you done anything interesting in the past few weeks – apart from watching TV or playing computer games? If the answer is 'no', you probably do not have a hobby or an interest in your life. So is it worth taking one up?

Hobbies can offer us different pleasures. To begin with, there is the enjoyment you get from doing something you find interesting. For example, if you collect stamps or coins, it is enjoyable to find new items to add to your collection and it is also satisfying to look through the ones you already have. Other hobbies, such as painting or pottery, allow us to be creative and we get pleasure from making something that we can feel proud of.

It is never too late to take up a new hobby. As we get older, we may become interested in subjects such as local history or gardening for the first time. We may even enjoy re-discovering an interest we had when we were younger.

So, if you sometimes feel there must be more to life than TV or the latest computer game, consider taking up a hobby!

Question 3

Dear Sir or Madam,

I am writing to apply for the position of waitress, which was recently advertised in the local newspaper.

I am eighteen years old and I am currently studying for a degree in Business Studies at university. For the past six months I have been working part-time as a waitress at Luigi's Italian Restaurant. Unfortunately, the restaurant is closing at the end of the month, which is why I am applying for this position.

I regard myself as hard-working and have had part-time jobs of different kinds since I was fourteen years old. I am responsible and enjoy dealing with customers. The skills I have learnt while working as a waitress mean I could be useful immediately and I wouldn't require a great deal of supervision.

As far as my interests are concerned, in my spare time I enjoy photography and I am a member of the Photography Society at university. I am also a keen amateur cook with an interest in international cuisine.

Please find enclosed my CV with details of people who would be happy to be contacted as referees, including my last employer.

Yours faithfully,

Maria Sanchez

Question 4

I spend a lot of time surfing the Internet and there are several websites that I use regularly. Some are useful for finding out information, and others for keeping up with the latest news. However, the site I use most is Twitter.

I enjoy web designing in my spare time and one of the main reasons I use the site is to connect with other people with the same interest. I follow other designers around the world, and being able to ask questions or for advice is invaluable. However, I also use Twitter to share advice of my own, like tips on how to design sites, and a lot of people follow me for this reason.

Twitter is particularly good for making local contacts, getting to know what's going on in your area and meeting people who live nearby. I go to a social media café once a month where I meet up with people I've contacted though Twitter.

I don't think Twitter is for everybody but if you want to feel more connected to your local community or would like to make professional contacts, it is very useful.

Acknowledgements

The Publisher and authors wish to thank the following rights holders for the use of copyright material:

Text from the following websites was adapted from data from the Office for National Statistics and licensed under the Open Government Licence v.1.0:

**Test 2: Reading and Use of English
(Part 1)**
http://ons.gov.uk/ons/dcp171776_309772.pdf

(Part 3)
http://www.ons.gov.uk/ons/rel/wellbeing/measuring-national-well-being/natural-environment/art-the-natural-environment.html#tab-Introduction

**Test 3: Reading and Use of English
(Part 1)**
http://ons.gov.uk/ons/rel/social-trends-rd/social-trends/social-trends-40/social-trends-40---transport-chapter.pdf

(Part 2)
http://ons.gov.uk/ons/dcp171776_306584.pdf

(Part 3)
http://ons.gov.uk/ons/rel/social-trends-rd/social-trends/social-trends-spotlight-on--e-society/art-social-trends---e-society.pdf

The following texts have been used under the Creative Commons Attributive License http://creativecommons.org/licenses/by/3.0/

**Test 2: Reading and Use of English
(Part 2)**
Sleep May Solve Grammar Gremlins By Souri Somphanith from http://blogs.plos.org/everyone/2013/06/07/sleep-may-solve-grammar-gremlins/

**Test 2: Reading and Use of English
(Part 6)**
Adapted text from http://blogs.plos.org/blog/2011/06/08/the-renaissance-man-how-to-become-a-scientist-over-and-over-again/ by Ed Yong reproduced by permission of the author

**Test 3: Reading and Use of English
(Part 6)**
Adapted text from http://blogs.plos.org/obesitypanacea/2013/07/04/physically-active-vacations-are-more-re-energizing by Travis Saunders

**Test 4: Reading and Use of English
(Part 1)**
Adapted text from Sharing was Caring for Ancient Humans and Their Prehistoric Pups by Michelle Dohm from http://blogs.plos.org/everyone/2013/05/28/sharing-was-caring-for-ancient-humans-and-their-prehistoric-pups/

**Test 4: Reading and Use of English
(Part 2)**
Adapted text from http://blogs.plos.org/globalhealth/2013/05/taking-care-of-yourself-is-not-very-manly-but-it-should-be/ by Alessandro Rhyl Demaio

Adapted text from the following reproduced by permission of Saudi Aramco World:

**Test 1: Reading and Use of English
(Part 6)**
http://www.saudiaramcoworld.com/issue/199704/spin.doctor.htm by Penny Parsekian Saudi Aramco World vol. 48 (4) July/August 1997

**Test 4: Reading and Use of English
(Part 6)**
http://www.saudiaramcoworld.com/issue/201104/one.card.at.a.time.htm by Piney Kesting Saudi Aramco World vol. 62 (4) July/August 2011

Adapted text from *Room Nineteen at the Montrose Club* by Fiona Joseph was reproduced by permission of the author and used in **Test 3: Reading and Use of English (Part 5)**.

If any copyright holders have been omitted, please contact the Publisher who will make the necessary arrangements at the first opportunity.

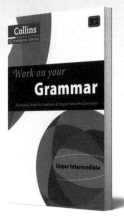

Collins Connect

Accessing the online test and training module

The Collins practice tests book for *Cambridge English: First* gives you access to a free online test and training module to help prepare you for the test.

> To access the online test and training module go to
> connect.collins.co.uk/ELT
> and follow the instructions.
>
> The access code is
>
> **7412FCE**

If you need any help with registering on Collins Connect, please contact us on

education.support@harpercollins.co.uk